Sea
Kayaker's
Pocket Guide

Shelley Johnson

Ragged Mountain Press / McGraw-Hill
Camden, Maine • New York • Chicago • San Francisco • Lisbon •
London • Madrid • Mexico City • Milan • New Delhi • San Juan •
Seoul• Singapore • Sydney • Toronto

Look for these other Ragged Mountain Press Pocket Guides:

Backpacker's Pocket Guide, Chris Townsend
Edible Wild Plants and Herbs, Alan M. Cvancara
Wilderness First Aid, Paul G. Gill Jr., M.D.

Ragged Mountain Press

A Division of The **McGraw-Hill** *Companies*

5 6 7 8 9 10 DOC/DOC 0 9 8 7 6
Copyright © 2002 Ragged Mountain Press
All rights reserved. The publisher takes no responsibility for the use of any of
the materials or methods described in this book, nor for the products thereof.
The name "Ragged Mountain Press" and the Ragged Mountain Press logo are
trademarks of The McGraw-Hill Companies. Printed in the United States of
America.

Library of Congress Cataloging-in-Publication Data
Johnson, Shelley, 1954–
    Sea kayaker's pocket guide / Shelley Johnson.
        p.   cm.–(A Ragged Mountain Press pocket guide)
Includes index.
    ISBN 0-07-137528-7 (alk. paper)
1. Sea kayaking.   I. Title.
    GV788.5.J63 2002
    797.1´224–dc21   2001003451

Questions regarding the content of this book should be addressed to
Ragged Mountain Press
P.O. Box 220
Camden, ME 04843
www.raggedmountainpress.com

Questions regarding the ordering of this book should be addressed to
The McGraw-Hill Companies
Customer Service Department
P.O. Box 547
Blacklick, OH 43004
Retail customers: 1-800-262-4729
Bookstores: 1-800-722-4726

This book is printed on 60# Citation by R. R. Donnelley
Photographs by Jim Dugan unless otherwise indicated. Photos on pages 27,
97 by the author; page 7 by NOAA; pages 42, 106, 107 (top), 136 by
www.arttoday.com; pages 38 (bottom), 39 (bottom), 67 by Nigel Calder;
pages 62, 63 by Bill Brogdon; pages 64, 85, 108, 109, 137 by Corbis Images;
page 74 by Ritchiesport; page 80 by Kim Downing; pages 86, 87, 88, 89 by
Doug Hayward; page 99 by Maine Island Trail Association; page 107 by U.S.
Fish and Wildlife Service; page 135 by Maine Forest Service.

Illustrations by Chris Hoyt; running foot illustration by Matt Watier; Design by
Geri Davis, Davis Associates, and Anton Marc; Production management by
Janet Robbins; Page layout by Deborah Evans; Edited by Tom McCarthy,
Jonathan Eaton, and Kate Thompson.

2nd Skin, 303 Aerospace Protectant, Aquaseal, Betadine, CoolMax, Cyalume,
Dr. Bronner's Magic Soap, Minicel, Popsicle, Shoe Goo, Slinky, Spenco, Steri-
Strip, Supplex, Vise-Grips, and WD-40 are registered trademarks.

Contents

Before You Go

Launch Day

On the Water

Before You Go

TRIP PLANNING

HAVING A PLAN

Any time you spend planning before a trip will be paid back many times over once you're under way. At the very least you need to plan your launch site, destination, and daily mileage.

Review your trip plan in relation to expected wind and tidal current information. Do you need to be aware of timing a particular tidal current or wind direction? Are there alternative routes that would provide better protection even if they add some mileage? What if you experience conditions different from those you expected—do you have a Plan B? Plan C or D?

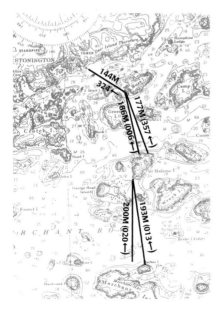

Think through scenarios that could occur and develop solutions for them. Note these solutions—you may need to use them while under way. It is far easier to utilize a well-thought-out backup plan than to scramble to develop one in a stressful situation.

Review your chart and begin to lay out your general course, noting places that provide wind protection and those that are exposed. Mark landing sites, bailout points, and overnight camping destinations on your chart. Record bearings (see page 68) and mileage for individual segments of your planned trip before leaving home. Begin to break your trip down into manageable pieces of 2 to 3 nautical miles and mark likely spots for rest breaks (see page 35, Pacing).

GETTING THE FORECAST

During the trip-planning phase, you can access weather information in a variety of ways: NOAA weather reports, local weather reports on radio and TV, and Internet sites. You should start this process several days prior to your departure date, since you'll need to determine what weather systems are moving in and out of your paddling area. Viewing weather and satellite maps will give you the "big picture." You can see developing systems and the approach of weather fronts.

NOAA weather reports are broadcast continuously on the weather band and can be picked up by any weather radio, VHF radio, and even some car radios. These broadcasts will give a marine weather report and data from offshore

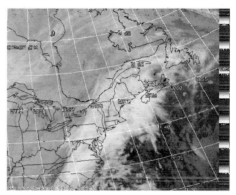

19 December 1996

20 December 1996

Review satellite weather images for developing patterns in the weather several days before your trip departure. Begin to develop your own forecast for your paddling area. The satellite images above represent two consecutive days of a weather front crossing New England.

buoys, though you might have to wait through the litany of inland reports first. NOAA weather reports are usually updated every three to four hours and are the best source for information on extreme weather, like the approach of a violent storm system or hurricane. You may also hear that a "small craft advisory" has been issued for your local waters. These advisories mean that strong winds of up to 33 knots are predicted—too strong for the average kayaker on open water.

You can get weather information off most news service Web sites, but the National Weather Service Web site (weather.gov or www.nos.noaa.gov) usually provides the most complete picture. For help in developing your own daily forecasts while under way, see Reading the Conditions, pages 38–45.

TIMING THE TIDE

When you plan a trip, consult a local tide table and record the time and height of low and high tide for each day you'll be paddling. You may need to make a correction from a reference station at a nearby town or coast guard station. Write the time for the high and low tides on your chartcase or on note cards that you can slip inside the case.

Now look at your planned landing and launch sites and see if the height and timing of the tide present any problems. You may have to adjust your site or the time of your arrival or departure because of the tides. Look at your planned route and backup routes. Are there any constrictions or areas where you will be faced with battling a strong tidal current? Will your

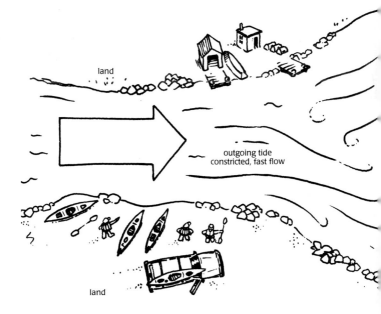

land

outgoing tide
constricted, fast flow

land

When a tidal current opposes the wind, waves will steepen and shorten.
This can be particularly dangerous at river mouths on a strong ebbing tide.

MARCH

		Bar Harbor		Rockland		Boothbay Hbr.		Portland	
		am	pm	am	pm	am	pm	am	pm
MONDAY		6:03 HI	6:54	6:17 HI	7:08	6:19 HI	7:10	6:25 HI	7:16
5		11.2 Height	10.0	10.4 Height	9.2	9.5 Height	8.3	9.7 Height	8.5
		— LO	12:43	— LO	12:52	12:01 LO	12:54	12:06 LO	12:59
		-- Height	0.0	— Height	0.0	1.0 Height	0.0	1.0 Height	0.0
		5:56 Sun	5:19	5:59 Sun	5:22	6:02 Sun	5:25	6:12 Sun	5:35
TUESDAY		7:10 HI	7:58	7:24 HI	8:12	7:26 HI	8:14	7:32 HI	8:20
6		11.6 Height	10.5	10.8 Height	9.7	9.9 Height	8.8	10.1 Height	9.0
		12:58 LO	1:48	1:07 LO	1:57	1:09 LO	1:59	1:14 LO	2:04
		0.6 Height	-0.5	0.6 Height	-0.5	0.6 Height	-0.5	0.6 Height	-0.5
		5:54 Sun	5:20	5:57 Sun	5:23	6:00 Sun	5:27	6:10 Sun	5:36
WEDNESDAY		8:14 HI	8:56	8:20 HI	9:10	8:30 HI	9:12	8:36 HI	9:18
7		12.1 Height	11.1	11.3 Height	10.3	10.4 Height	9.4	10.6 Height	9.6
		2:02 LO	2:47	2:11 LO	2:56	2:13 LO	2:58	2:18 LO	3:03
		0.1 Height	-1.0	0.1 Height	-1.0	0.1 Height	-1.0	0.1 Height	-1.0
		5:52 Sun	5:21	5:55 Sun	5:24	5:58 Sun	5:27	6:08 Sun	5:37
THURSDAY		9:13 HI	9:50	9:27 HI	10:04	9:29 HI	10:06	9:35 HI	10:12
8		12.5 Height	11.7	11.7 Height	10.9	10.8 Height	10.0	10.8 Height	10.2
		3:02 LO	3:41	3:11 LO	3:50	3:13 LO	3:52	3:18 LO	3:57
		-0.5 Height	-1.4	-0.5 Height	-1.4	-0.5 Height	-1.4	-0.5 Height	-1.4
		5:50 Sun	5:23	5:53 Sun	5:26	5:56 Sun	5:29	6:06 Sun	5:39

Note the low and high tides for your area.

wind

opposition of forces will steepen waves, shorten troughs

out to sea

plans put you in opposition to this tidal current and, if so, at what stage of the tidal flow (beginning, middle, or end)? Are there any strong tidal currents that might oppose the predicted wind directions during your trip? For example, you do not want to be at the mouth of a powerful river during the middle of an ebb tide with a breeze blowing hard up the river. These are potentially dangerous conditions. Remember that tidal flow is strongest during the middle two hours as it moves from high to low water and from low to high water. Adjust your plans to take into account the answers to these questions. Timing the tide can make a huge difference in the safety and convenience of your trip. So, take a close look at your tide tables and study the tidal current tables or tidal current charts if you are unfamiliar with the area. Then review your chart and decide on the best routes with the most advantageous conditions. After all, timing is everything.

CLOTHING AND EQUIPMENT

STAYING WARM, STAYING DRY

The best way to stay warm is to stay completely dry. A dry suit will help you do this by encasing you in waterproof material (it may be a breathable membrane as well) with latex gaskets at the openings for wrists, ankles, and neck. But a dry suit isn't always needed or affordable. Combining layers of insulation, wicking fabrics, and waterproof and windproof materials may be the best approach, since it allows you the flexibility of shedding and donning layers as needed.

There are two ways you'll get wet on the water: rain and spray over the deck of your boat, and immersion. It is very tempting to deal only with the possibility of rough or wet weather and assume that immersion is an unlikely event. And it usually is. But it is far safer to dress for the possibility of immersion than to be caught unprepared and pay the potentially serious consequences. After all, it's pretty easy to cool down when you're surrounded by cold water, but it's difficult to warm up when you're in the water or exposed to the wind while you're soaking wet (see Hypothermia, pages 130–31).

Neoprene is a closed-cell material that provides buoyancy and warmth even when immersed. Most of the wet suits used by paddlers are 3 mm thick, though wet suits range from 0.5 to 5.0 mm. The thicker the wet suit, the greater its insulating power.

Avoid all-cotton clothing, since it will cool you down rapidly and becomes heavy when wet. Wool will work as an insulating layer, though it gets cumbersome when wet. In a pinch, trash bags will work as an outer layer to protect you from getting wet, though you may get pretty steamy inside. Don't forget to cover your head; you lose most of your heat from the top of your head. A wool or fleece hat works well.

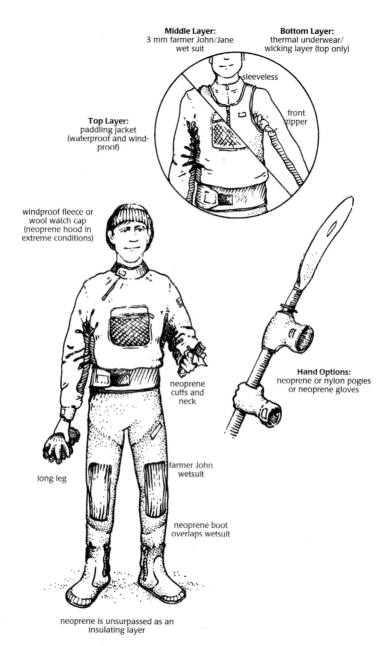

Middle Layer: 3 mm farmer John/Jane wet suit

Bottom Layer: thermal underwear/wicking layer (top only)

sleeveless

front zipper

Top Layer: paddling jacket (waterproof and wind-proof)

windproof fleece or wool watch cap (neoprene hood in extreme conditions)

neoprene cuffs and neck

Hand Options: neoprene or nylon pogies or neoprene gloves

long leg

farmer John wetsuit

neoprene boot overlaps wetsuit

neoprene is unsurpassed as an insulating layer

Basic clothing layers should include synthetic fabrics next to the skin, an intermediate layer for insulation, and a top layer that is waterproof and windproof.

STAYING COOL

Many of us take to the water to cool off, but we still need to protect ourselves from the fierce rays of the sun. You can shield yourself from the sun with fabric or by slathering yourself with sunscreen.

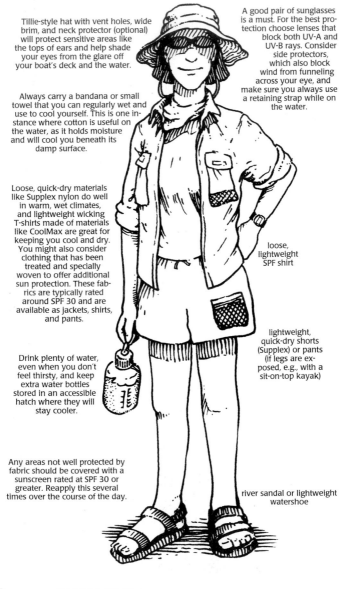

Tillie-style hat with vent holes, wide brim, and neck protector (optional) will protect sensitive areas like the tops of ears and help shade your eyes from the glare off your boat's deck and the water.

Always carry a bandana or small towel that you can regularly wet and use to cool yourself. This is one instance where cotton is useful on the water, as it holds moisture and will cool you beneath its damp surface.

Loose, quick-dry materials like Supplex nylon do well in warm, wet climates, and lightweight wicking T-shirts made of materials like CoolMax are great for keeping you cool and dry. You might also consider clothing that has been treated and specially woven to offer additional sun protection. These fabrics are typically rated around SPF 30 and are available as jackets, shirts, and pants.

Drink plenty of water, even when you don't feel thirsty, and keep extra water bottles stored in an accessible hatch where they will stay cooler.

Any areas not well protected by fabric should be covered with a sunscreen rated at SPF 30 or greater. Reapply this several times over the course of the day.

A good pair of sunglasses is a must. For the best protection choose lenses that block both UV-A and UV-B rays. Consider side protectors, which also block wind from funneling across your eye, and make sure you always use a retaining strap while on the water.

loose, lightweight SPF shirt

lightweight, quick-dry shorts (Supplex) or pants (if legs are exposed, e.g., with a sit-on-top kayak)

river sandal or lightweight watershoe

LIFE VESTS (PFDs)

A life vest won't do you much good if you've tucked it under the deck rigging. These days, life vests are comfortable and low profile, so you have little excuse for not wearing yours. Most kayaking vests are type 3 life vests, which are designed for the recreational market. They are cut short so they don't ride up when you're seated and can be adjusted for a snug fit so they remain in place whether you're in or out of the water.

Check your life vest each season for signs of UV damage that may have weakened the fabric and created tears. The fabric is important for protecting the foam underneath. If this foam is exposed to UV it will rapidly degrade and lose its buoyancy. You can treat your life vest's fabric with 303 Aerospace Protectant, a UV-inhibiting compound, to slow this process.

High-visibility colors (orange, lime, yellow) are best on the water. For added visibility add some retroreflective tape; you can buy this by the foot at paddle-sports shops and marine chandleries.

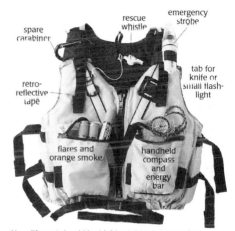

spare carabiner

rescue whistle

emergency strobe

tab for knife or small flash-light

retro-reflective tape

flares and orange smoke

handheld compass and energy bar

Your life vest should be highly visible and should be adjustable for a snug fit all around. Signaling devices and small pieces of gear can be carried on or in your life vest.

When you don your life vest, make sure it is properly fitted. Snug down all compression straps and zip up the vest fully. Have someone try to lift you by the shoulders. The vest should remain in place and not pull up under your chin. Remember, when the vest is wet, it will loosen.

CHECKING YOUR GEAR

Before you begin the final stages of planning and packing, go over your gear and look for signs of wear and tear that could spell trouble while under way.

Use a handheld compass to check your deck compass for accuracy. Bubbles or cracks in the housing may cause inaccurate readings Once your boat is packed, check again to avoid any compass deviation caused by nearby ferrous objects like batteries or cookware.

KAYAK	torn or frayed deck rigging, hatch straps, or carrying toggles
	rudder or skeg jams
	torn or cracked hatch gaskets or covers
	structural damage to hull, deck, bulkheads, or hatches
	jammed or damaged foot braces or rudder tracks
SPRAYSKIRTS	peeling seam tape
	malfunctioning adjustments for waist and cockpit size
	poorly attached grab loop
PADDLE	cracks along the paddle shaft
	malfunctioning joint on a two-piece paddle
	water trapped in the blades
BILGE PUMP	bent pump shaft
	torn diaphragm
	torn or missing float collar
PADDLE FLOAT	malfunctioning valve
	corroded hardware
	tears or pinholes in bladder
LIFE VEST	malfunctioning zippers
	fabric tears
COMPASS	bubbles present or loss of liquid
	cracks in the housing

ADJUSTING THE FIT

Seat and Cockpit Bring your seatback or backband into position so that it supports your back and keeps you from slouching in your seat. Make sure your lower back is pushed into the back of the seat base and your upper legs are lifted slightly and supported by the front edge of your seat (add a piece of foam or rolled towel to help support the backs of your thighs). If you prefer a snug fit, add pieces of foam alongside your hips or under the deck for better lower-body control of your kayak (tape these into place and later glue them for a permanent adjustment).

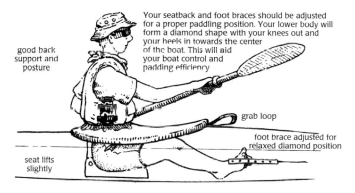

good back support and posture

Your seatback and foot braces should be adjusted for a proper paddling position. Your lower body will form a diamond shape with your knees out and your heels in towards the center of the boat. This will aid your boat control and paddling efficiency

grab loop

foot brace adjusted for relaxed diamond position

seat lifts slightly

Foot Braces The balls of your feet should rest comfortably on the foot brace pedals with your lower body forming a relaxed diamond shape. You should never strain to reach the foot pedals or have your ankle bent in an uncomfortable position.

Sprayskirt The waist tunnel on your sprayskirt should allow for adjustments in both height (it may have suspenders) and diameter. Cinch the waist snugly around you and adjust the suspenders before you put on your life vest. The waist tunnel should sit high enough on your upper body so that the deck of your sprayskirt sheds water rather than allowing it to pool above your lap once you're seated in the boat. Make sure the skirt doesn't pull free of the rear coaming when you lean forward. The sprayskirt deck should fit snugly around the coaming but be easily detached from the coaming with a quick yank on the grab loop. Make sure the grab loop is large enough to slip your hand into and accessible at all times.

PRETRIP DETAILS

WHO TO CONTACT

It's always reassuring to have a list of emergency contacts in case things go terribly wrong. Include a list of these numbers inside your chartcase or taped to the back of a VHF radio or cellular phone (see page 82 for more on use of VHF radios). Make sure everyone in your party knows where these numbers are recorded and how to operate the cell phone or radio they would use to place these calls.

A laminated card attached to your VHF radio should include your call sign, emergency contact numbers, and local call channels. Also consider including the basics of the VHF Distress Call Protocol (at top).

In addition to 911, the following numbers could prove useful:

Nearest coast guard station

State police

Poison Control Center

Nearest hospital

Contact number for marine mammal strandings

Contact number for information on red tide closures or other restrictions on shellfish harvesting

BEFORE YOU GO

FLOAT PLAN

It's one thing to get away, but it's an entirely different matter when nobody knows where you've gone! Always leave a float plan with a family member, friend, or neighbor. The float plan isn't designed to regiment your movements; it's to let people on shore know where you've gone paddling and when you're expected back. For a multiday trip, you might want to include a copy of your chart with marks showing each of your planned stops and overnight locations.

Some public and private launch sites require that you file a float plan; others offer this service to small boaters. Many paddling clubs also have a float plan network available by phone or computer. Don't forget to close out your float plan once you complete your trip or if your plans get canceled.

Float Plan

Boat description: Current Designs Solstice, bright yellow; Sisuitl (tandem), white; Sealution, teal, ...

Members of party: Shelley, Vaughan, Molly, Ken . . . .

Day, time, and location of launch: Monday July 23, 7:00 am, Stonington (behind ferry) . . . .

Car/Cars license plate number, location, and description: Jeep, 42kayak4, Sierra p/u, JL125U, Stonington boat launch (parking at Steve's garage) . . . .

Day, time, and location of return: Wednesday July 25, 3pm, Stonington

VHF call sign . . . . Cell phone number . . . .

Day: July 23 . . . . . Planned locations: Steve's I.—camp; Harbor I.—camp
. . . . Will call to check in: 8pm . . . .

Day: July 24 . . . . . Planned locations: Wheat I.—camp (explore Isle au Haut) . . . .
. . . . Will call to check in: 8pm . . . .

Day: July 25 . . . . . Planned locations: Return Stonington . . . .

Should arrive home or call to check in: 5pm . . . .

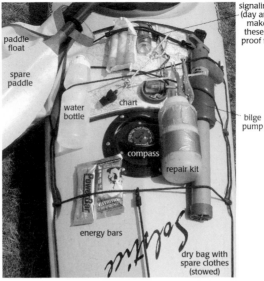

paddle float

spare paddle

water bottle

chart

compass

energy bars

signaling devices (day and night—make one of these a waterproof flashlight)

bilge pump

repair kit

dry bag with spare clothes (stowed)

TEN ESSENTIALS

Any packing list will evolve to fit your own quirks and actual paddling plans. But there are essentials (in addition to a paddle, life vest, and a sprayskirt for decked boats) that are just that—things you automatically grab whenever you go paddling. Consider keeping the essentials packed in a mesh bag so all you need to do is grab it and go.

Obviously, a multiday trip will require more and varied gear, but your essentials bag may often be sufficient for day trips and serve as the base for your longer trip packing strategy.

---

10 Essentials Checklist

Paddle float ✓

Spare paddle ✓

Water bottles (filled) ✓

Chart ✓

Compass ✓ compare to deck compass for accuracy

Repair kit ✓ duct tape, screws, bolts, etc.

Energy bars ✓

Bilge pump ✓

Signaling devices ✓ day and night, waterproof flashlight

Dry bag with spare clothes ✓ anorak, wool hat, etc.

ORGANIZING YOUR GEAR

There's nothing like pulling into a campsite after a long day of paddling and being able to go on automatic pilot as you set up camp and prepare the evening meal. Conversely, there is nothing more frustrating than having to root around in every dry bag and dump their entire contents on the ground because you can't find the toilet paper or that evening's entrée.

After you've planned your menu for the trip, repackage all the food and spices into small bags and then combine these smaller packages into the meal bag for a specific day and label it as such. Store spices and utensils that are used with almost every meal in the general kitchen bag. When you repackage food, you are jettisoning all the excess packaging—and weight—that you would otherwise have to carry with you until a garbage can comes along. Clip cooking instructions or dietary information from the packaging if needed and place them inside the bags. Precut vegetables and prepare salad dressings and other sauces in advance to keep things simple at the end of the day.

Organize gear and supplies by category: kitchen gear, meals, liquids, latrine gear, clothing, camp gear, repair materials, cleaning supplies, group safety gear, and special gear (books, stargazing charts, harmonica, etc.)

Make sure you know what's in every dry bag. You can use a color-coded system so you can see at a glance which bags contain, for example, kitchen items. Or simply label the outside of the bag with duct tape and a waterproof marker. Stick to your system when you repack, and you'll always be able to find things when you need them.

Launch Day

TRANSPORTING KAYAKS

KAYAKS ON CARS

There are numerous ways to carry boats on vehicles, from high tech to homegrown solutions. A kayak needs to be supported in at least two places by something that will conform to the shape of the boat's hull or shoulder and will absorb some of the jolts from the road. You'll need to strap or tie your kayak to this support system and then make sure it is attached to a car rack or your car. You should also consider using a bow and stern line that you tie to something solid at each end of your vehicle (this can be challenging in this age of plastic bumpers).

Don't use cheap line salvaged from the dump. Instead, buy $\frac{3}{16}$- to $\frac{5}{16}$-inch static (nonstretch) line or use tie-down straps, which don't require knots. To minimize strap humming, add a few twists before tightening.

Make sure anything you are carrying in your boat is secured and all hatches are in place. A cockpit cover with a tether strap comes in handy in rainy weather and keeps gear stored in the cockpit from flying out. Check your boat and lines periodically and remember to glance up or back to see if the boat seems secure while under way. If you're traveling in strong winds, consider adding a perimeter line—a backup line that encircles the boat and becomes its support system in case another line parts (breaks) or a strap gives way.

When you load your boat, don't be intimidated by to pick it up and position it on the roof of your car. You only need to work with one end at a time, and you can break things into small, more easily managed steps. A short stepladder is handy for tall vehicles, and a piece of carpet or bathroom mat is invaluable when loading over the back of a vehicle.

tie stern with taut-line hitch

tie-down straps

tie bow with taut-line hitch

Your vehicle's style and size may determine placement of cradles and straps. Make all lines and straps snug but don't overtighten and cause dimpling (plastic kayaks) or fractures (composite kayaks).

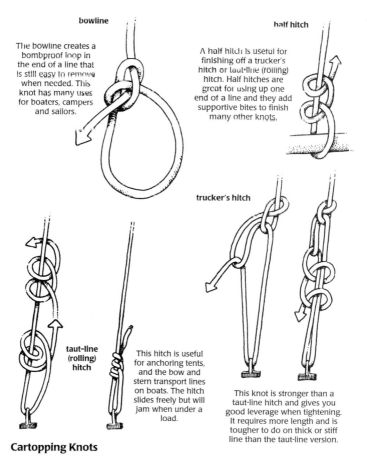

bowline

The bowline creates a bombproof loop in the end of a line that is still easy to remove when needed. This knot has many uses for boaters, campers and sailors.

half hitch

A half hitch is useful for finishing off a trucker's hitch or taut-line (rolling) hitch. Half hitches are great for using up one end of a line and they add supportive bites to finish many other knots.

trucker's hitch

taut-line (rolling) hitch

This hitch is useful for anchoring tents, and the bow and stern transport lines on boats. The hitch slides freely but will jam when under a load.

This knot is stronger than a taut-line hitch and gives you good leverage when tightening. It requires more length and is tougher to do on thick or stiff line than the taut-line version.

Cartopping Knots

CARRYING YOUR KAYAK

To get your kayak to the water by yourself:

1. Bend your knees (not your back) and grab the closest edge of the cockpit and slide the boat up your leg until it rests on your thigh.

2. Grasp the boat on either side of the cockpit coaming and roll one edge of the cockpit over to your lowered shoulder.

3. Stand up straight and balance the boat on your shoulder.

As you walk with your boat on your shoulder, make sure to use both hands to stabilize the boat in any wind. If the coaming digs into your shoulder, use a life vest for protection. When you are ready to lay the boat down, simply reverse your steps, gradually lowering the boat to your thigh and then to the ground.

Sea kayaks are often too unwieldy to solo carry—there's just too much boat hanging out at either end. It is usually easier to position a person at either end of the boat and make use of the carrying toggles anchored to the boat at the bow and stern. You should still cup your hand under the boat as a backup, since toggles have been known to break or slip out of a person's hand.

Kayak carts, or trolleys, offer a great way to move your boat to and from the water. These handy sets of wheels can attach over the stern of the boat or sit amidships for an easy roll down to the water. The advantage of using a cart is that you can carry a fully loaded boat or throw your gear in the cockpit for one trip. Most models fold up to fit in a hatch in case you want to carry your cart along for the day. Make sure the cart is padded so that the boat is protected from the jolts of rough terrain.

TRIMMING AND PACKING THE BOAT

"Trimming the boat" means making sure it rides evenly in the water. It shouldn't list from side to side or be significantly lower at either the bow or stern. Once you've loaded your boat, always check the trim both with and without you in the cockpit. It is much easier to make corrections to your load before launching than when under way.

Keep your deck clear of unneeded clutter. You don't want the high center of gravity or the exposure to wind that a heavily cluttered deck creates. You also need to be careful to keep safety gear such as your paddle float, bilge pump, and signaling devices close at hand and reachable from the cockpit or the

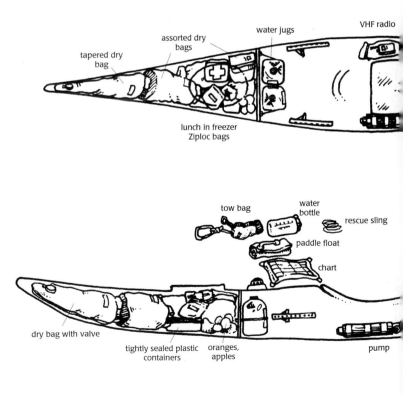

tapered dry bag · assorted dry bags · water jugs · VHF radio · lunch in freezer Ziploc bags

tow bag · water bottle · rescue sling · paddle float · chart · dry bag with valve · tightly sealed plastic containers · oranges, apples · pump water. Check to make sure that no deck items will hinder the easy release of your sprayskirt or prevent you from reentering the boat from the water.

In general, you'll want to load heavy items low and close to the center and centerline of the boat. A top-heavy kayak has a tendency to roll; a low center of gravity will give you a far more stable arrangement. Keeping heavier items close to the center of the boat allows the bow and stern to ride a bit higher and make their way through waves more easily. Balancing the boat along its centerline keeps the boat from listing to one side and demanding constant corrective strokes when under way.

Make sure heavy items are well secured and will not suddenly shift if you lean the boat on edge. Carry water in several small containers instead of one large one; this will allow you more flexibility in packing. Soft-sided water carriers are handy since they conform to a space and are easily secured in place with other gear. As you use up provisions over the course of the trip, you can capture air in a dry bag if needed to help hold other gear in place.

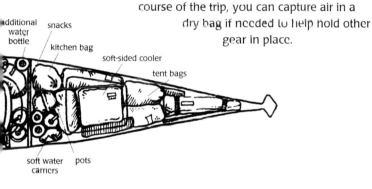

additional water bottle · snacks · kitchen bag · soft-sided cooler · tent bags · soft water carriers · pots

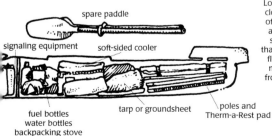

spare paddle · signaling equipment · soft-sided cooler · fuel bottles water bottles backpacking stove · tarp or groundsheet · poles and Therm-a-Rest pad

Load heavy items first. Place them close to the center and centerline of your boat and make sure they are secured in place. Packing in several small containers rather than one large one gives you more flexibility in packing. Throw in a mesh bag for transporting gear from your kayak to the campsite.

LAUNCH SITE CHECKLIST

The earlier stages of your trip planning should have produced a thorough checklist of all the items you'll need. If you're just out for a day trip, these might not be more than the ten essentials on page 18. If you are heading out for a multiday trip, you will need a detailed accounting of whether items are present and packed.

Do not simply scan your list and assure yourself that everything is in place. Check off items as you pack them. If you don't lay eyes on it, it doesn't get checked off the list. Investigate each dry bag and consider noting what is in each as you check things off. This may save you some aggravation when you're ready to set up camp at the end of the day.

In addition to your complete packing list, use a launch site checklist to ensure you haven't forgotten to do something crucial. Before paddling away, review your launch site checklist with all group members. Make sure everyone knows who has which pieces of the group's safety gear. Review group signals and paddling formations before setting out (see Group Travel, page 46).

Launch Site Checklist

Vehicle locked and properly parked ✓

Car keys (under left rear bumper/spare in first-aid kit)

Water bottles filled ✓

Float plan filed ✓ check in w/ Barb tomorrow night

Who has:

>VHF — Jim
>
>Cell phone — Sally and Jeff
>
>First-aid kit — Linda
>
>Repair kit — Jim
>
>Towlines — Jim and Linda

Check:

>Hatches secured ✓
>
>Boat trim ✓
>
>Compass deviation ✓

Other:

Sunscreen! ✓

Don't forget to set GPS launch waypoint.

For channel crossing let Jim lead — Linda sweep

Make sure Jeff packed his Epi-Pen (where?)

GETTING IN AND OUT OF YOUR KAYAK

AT THE BEACH

Getting in and out of your boat can be a fine balancing act, resulting in a graceful entry or exit or an embarrassing spill that has you starting your trip wet and flustered. You need to create a support system that holds the boat in place and gives you stability as you crawl in and out. You can use your paddle and the shoreline to create the support you need.

Place your paddle behind the cockpit coaming and extend it out perpendicular to the boat. Let the far paddle blade rest on the bottom or on some piece of shore. Now squat next to the boat and, making sure the paddle is held firmly in place, sit on the edge of the boat, place first one foot and then the other into the cockpit, and slide in. One hand should be behind your back and clamping the paddle shaft to the coaming; the other hand will be on the paddle shaft where the bulk of your weight will rest. This arrangement will anchor the boat to the paddle and the paddle to solid shore. Otherwise the boat might slide away from you as you try to enter or be too unstable for you to get seated. To exit your boat, simply reverse the procedure.

Make sure the back of the paddle blade is grounded on the bottom or a piece of shore and held firmly in place perpendicular to your kayak.

Lean on the grounded paddle for support while you tuck your feet into the cockpit. The boat will be held in place by your paddle.

LAUNCHING AND LANDING AT A DOCK

A dock gives you a solid object for holding your boat in place while you enter and exit. Ideally, the dock is close to the water, making it easy to set up the support system in which you use your paddle perpendicular to your boat to hold everything in place. Unfortunately, docks aren't always positioned so conveniently.

If the dock is much higher than your boat, you won't be able to use your paddle for support. Instead you'll have to make a careful transfer of your weight into and out of the boat. Align your boat parallel to the dock, swing your legs over the edge of the dock, and hold the boat with your foot. Now turn onto your belly and begin to slide your weight down into the cockpit, keeping your arms on the dock and using them to maintain your balance. Once the bulk of your weight is over the center of the cockpit, lower your upper body into the boat while keeping a firm grip on the dock with both hands. As you seat yourself in the cockpit, keep one hand resting on the dock for support until you are completely settled. Re-

Using both hands, transfer your weight from your cockpit to the dock (or dock to cockpit).

Keep your feet in the cockpit until you are seated on the dock and can secure your boat.

verse these steps if you are landing at a dock.

If there are others around the dock, it is helpful to have someone hold the boat alongside the dock. You might also consider tying your boat to cleats on the dock, but you will need someone to release the lines once you are seated.

LAUNCHING IN SURF

Before you throw yourself into the uncertainties of launching through surf, take the time to observe the waves that are breaking along the length of the launch site. Locate areas where the break seems gentler and places where the overlap of breaks creates a turbulent soup. Now begin to time the interval between wave breaks and see if you can ascertain any pattern to the wave sets. Is one wave per set bigger or smaller than the others? Use this information to time your actual launch.

Make sure you are ready to go before you position your boat at the water's edge and enter the cockpit. This is not the time to realize your paddle is just out of reach or a hatch cover is not secured. Attach your sprayskirt and then use your hands to scoot out into the next break until your boat is afloat. Be careful to avoid being hit by a wave and washed sideways back up the beach. You may make a false start or two, but keep trying to be quick about getting in and ready to paddle forward.

Paddle aggressively through the surf and keep a wary eye out so you don't get caught at the base of a wave as it begins to break. Try to punch through the waves and present as small a profile as possible to the wave face. If a wave begins to break over you, get your paddle alongside the boat and bend your upper body forward to spear through the wave. You don't want to take a direct hit on your chest or exposed paddle blade. Once you feel the wave pass, resume paddling until you're outside the surf zone. Once there, you can remove any water from your cockpit and make sure that any items on deck are still secure.

If at any point you begin to be surfed backward down a wave face, use your paddle as a bow rudder to keep the boat pointed directly out. You want to avoid broaching and being sent back to the beach.

rudder up

Use your hands and paddle blade (gently!) to scoot toward the water until you are afloat. Make sure you are ready to go and pointed perpendicular to the waves.

On the Water

PADDLING SMART

PADDLE GRIP

How you handle your paddle says a lot about you as a kayaker. Out on the water you'll see everything from anxious death grips to nonchalant handshakes. Paddle grip is about control and comfort. You should never overgrip your paddle, which would be like doing an isometric exercise with your paddle over the course of the day. A delicate grip will keep your wrist straight and the back of your hand aligned with your forearm. A too-tight grip and side-to-side movement of the wrist are the most common causes of wrist pain in paddlers (see page 122). You can avoid this by keeping your pinkies away from the shaft.

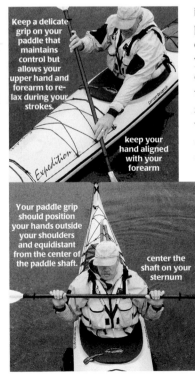

Keep a delicate grip on your paddle that maintains control but allows your upper hand and forearm to relax during your strokes.

keep your hand aligned with your forearm

Your paddle grip should position your hands outside your shoulders and equidistant from the center of the paddle shaft.

center the shaft on your sternum

Many paddles have oval areas or even rubber grips that help with the precise placement of the hands in a comfortable position. Check yourself frequently over the course of the day to make sure your hands haven't traveled along the paddle shaft so that your grip is out of kilter.

MOVING FORWARD

Your torso is the engine that drives your forward stroke. Your arms merely serve to connect the paddle to this engine as it rotates from side to side. Getting this concept ingrained will make your paddling much more efficient and allow you to paddle farther and longer without tiring. You need to get used to using the larger muscles of your back and abdomen, rather than the short muscles of your arms. It is technique, not brute strength, that is key to paddling efficiently for sea kayakers.

Hold your paddle well away from your body (imagine having something really smelly smeared on the shaft) and squared with your shoulders and chest. Now rotate your torso to plant a paddle blade in the water; then uncoil your torso to push the upper hand and drive the stroke. Try to develop an easy cadence that you can maintain for twenty minutes or more without pausing. Imagine a bell attached to your belly button. It would ring with each stroke as your torso rotates from side to side.

Your forward stroke is a repetitive motion you will use to click off the miles during a day of paddling. It needs to be relaxed and fluid.

Your upper hand should not be more than chin high unless you are uncorking a power stroke in a sprint. Instead, keep a fairly low angle to your forward stroke and make your movements fluid. This may not seem natural at first; you'll be tempted to "bicycle" with your arms. Keep practicing until you smooth out the rough spots. You'll be a far more graceful and powerful kayaker if you do.

The blade should exit the water alongside your hip, and your torso should be parallel with the paddle shaft throughout the stroke.

TURNING (SWEEP STROKES)

You can turn a kayak by making strokes on only one side of the boat. If you continue to paddle only on the right, the boat will turn to the left. But you can make your turns quicker and more powerful by reaching out from the boat in a sweeping motion that starts up by your foot and ends at the stern. It is very important that you square your torso with the paddle shaft and watch the entire stroke. You don't want to lose sight of the blade before it exits the water, since it is easy for the boat to trip over the paddle blade at the stern.

lean your boat on edge to shorten the waterline and make your sweep stroke more effective

watch the blade as it moves through the water and keep your chest parallel with the paddle shaft

If you shorten the waterline of your boat by leaning it on edge, your turning strokes will be noticeably more effective. This will require you to lift a knee and hip to bring the boat up on its shoulder as you lean into the stroke. Since it would be handy to have some support throughout this boat lean, angle the paddle blade so it's somewhat flatter to the water. This will give the leading edge of the blade a rising angle (similar to a sweep roll) and give you some support if you begin to tip in that direction.

You can make turning strokes from the bow (forward sweep) or from the stern (reverse sweep), depending on whether you wish to stop all forward momentum or just correct its direction a bit. You can also combine a forward and a reverse sweep stroke (on opposite sides) to turn your boat around within a confined area.

PACING

The details of your trip may determine the timing and frequency of your rest stops, but try to schedule plenty of these into any trip plan. Look at your planned course and break it into smaller segments of 2 to 3 nautical miles. This will usually be the average distance you'll travel in one hour at an easy touring pace. (See page 72 for determining your speed of travel.)

Build in at least one rest stop per hour to provide plenty of opportunities to regroup, monitor weather and other VHF broadcasts, break out water and snacks, make any needed gear or clothing adjustments, and review trip plans. You may even choose to take quick breathers between rest stops, assuming that strong winds or currents are not a factor.

The perfect rest stop will provide wind protection and be out of any opposing current or challenging conditions. A pocket cove or shoal to park your boat stern in is ideal, but you can make do by grabbing any accessible piece of shoreline to hold a position. If you are taking a break during a long crossing, consider rafting up with other group members and setting a sea anchor off the bow (not in heavy boat traffic). Being able to sit quietly for a few minutes is invaluable if you will need to review your trip plans and make adjustments while under way.

Pulling into a protected piece of water is a great time for group members to check in with one another, have some water and snacks, and review their next trip segment.

CROSSING A CURRENT (FERRYING)

Ferrying is a whitewater technique for crossing rivers without being pushed downstream. The kayaker points the boat upstream and sets a bow angle so that the downstream current pushes the boat across the river. All the paddler has to do is set a stern rudder to keep the boat properly aligned.

Sea kayakers can make use of ferrying, too. But instead of a downstream current, we are faced with a tidal current that changes over time. We also have to factor wind into the equation. Often it is the wind (and the seas it creates), not the tidal current, that we are playing off of when we set our ferry angle.

If you want to cross a channel, you will rarely find it practical to paddle directly across to your destination. Instead, you will need to point up into the wind and/or current and ferry across the channel, monitoring your progress in relation to landmarks. If you were to ignore the wind and current, you would be pushed below your destination and face a hard paddle into the wind or current to reach your landing site. In poor visibility, it is useful to set an even more severe angle so you arrive across the channel above your intended destination. Then you can turn and coast to your destination using the shoreline to stay found. See also Tidal Current Calculations, pages 76–77.

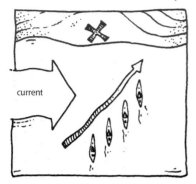

paddling a compass heading

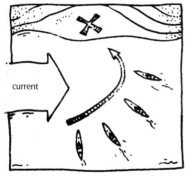

"aiming" at destination

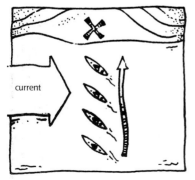

correcting for current

ON THE WATER

STAYING ON COURSE

Sometimes you may find that as you paddle forward your path is more of a "snake-wake" than a smooth, efficient line of travel. The last thing you want to do is lose momentum by stopping and turning to make a course correction. It would be far easier to maintain your forward momentum and make corrections while under way. You'll need to get used to looking ahead and monitoring your boat's progress and automatically making these corrections, which you can do with a mere shift of your weight in the cockpit.

If you lift your hip and thigh on one side of the boat, the other side will be lowered and a bit heavier as it rides through the water. If you continue to paddle forward, you'll find that the boat begins to turn away from the side that is slightly lower and heavier. This is not a deep lean or decisive turning movement. Instead, it is a means to keep your boat on course with slight corrections while maintaining your forward momentum.

tree behind dock makes range

Learn to make these corrections automatically and smoothly without changing the cadence of your paddling. These adjustments should be as instinctive as knowing where to place your foot as you climb a set of stairs. You'll be saved a lot of effort and look far more graceful on the water once you really groove this technique.

shift body weight

Look ahead to landmarks (preferably ranges) as you paddle. Make minor course corrections by shifting your weight in the cockpit as you paddle forward.

READING THE CONDITIONS

CLOUD TYPES

Winds and temperatures can be felt, but clouds are the visible signposts of weather. Clouds are beautiful in their own right, but it is their usefulness as weather indicators that makes them important to kayakers. The movement, sequence, color, and shape of clouds can tell us what is brewing in the weather. Clouds are named by their altitude and shape, as they swap prefixes and suffixes with abandon.

Cirrus: These are the highest clouds and the earliest indicators of approaching weather. They form wispy trails across the skies that speak of turbulence aloft. They may thicken to indicate the approach of warmer, moist air as they morph into stratus clouds that hold rain or snow.

Cumulus: These puffy, towering clouds may range from the purest white to a dirty gray. A parade of discrete white altocumulus (midaltitude cumulus) clouds is typical of pleasant summer weather. When they begin to gang up and their mood darkens into stratocumulus (layered cumulus) clouds, keep a wary eye out. Cumulus clouds may turn into violent **cumulonimbus** clouds, or thunderheads, that tower over the landscape with their signature anvil shape. If you see one of these monsters headed your way, get off the water.

Stratus: These clouds create thick cover that can block the sun and at best bring unsettled conditions. They are usually part of a lowering and darkening of the cloud cover that brings rain or snow. Their layered sheets help define other cloud formations as they make their mark on the naming process with a *strato* prefix or *stratus* suffix.

Nimbus: These are clouds looking to pick a fight. They have ragged, dark edges and often pour rain that is heavy enough to obscure visibility. They form thick cover as **nimbostratus** clouds and completely block the sun. When they form the rolling edge of an approaching thunderhead, or cumulonimbus cloud (shown at right), watch out.

BEAUFORT SCALE (WIND SPEED TABLE)

Developed in 1808, this scale of wind forces was used to describe the effect wind would have on a full-rigged frigate under sail. Today the Beaufort Scale includes wind speeds in addition to the Beaufort system of "forces." The beauty of the Beaufort Scale is that it outlines what you can expect to see on land and water at different wind velocities and, conversely, it links your own observations to a particular wind speed.

Beaufort number	Wind speed (knots)	Wind description	Water description	Land description
0	less than one knot	calm	flat calm	nothing stirring
1	1–3	light air	ripples	smoke drifts gently according to wind direction
2	4–6	light breeze	small wavelets	air movement can be felt on your face
3	7–10	gentle breeze	scattered whitecaps and large wavelets	leaves and twigs in motion
4	11–16	moderate breeze	lots of whitecaps; small waves lengthen	loose paper blows around; small branches move
5	17–21	fresh breeze	mostly whitecaps with spray; moderate waves	flags ripple; small trees begin to sway
6	22–27	strong breeze	whitecaps everywhere; more spray	larger trees and branches move; whistling heard in sailboat rigging
7	28–33	near gale	foam from waves begins blowing in streaks; sea heaps up	whole tree sways; your skirt gets blown up around your face
8	34–40	gale	foam is blown in well-defined streaks; crests begin breaking	branches and twigs torn from trees; you have trouble making headway on foot
9	41–47	strong gale	dense streaking; spray reduces visibility	roof shingles peeled from houses
10	48–55	storm	sea begins to roll and look white; spray reduces visibility	trees uprooted; structural damage to buildings
11	56–63	violent storm	sea covered with white foam patches; large waves	widespread damage
12	64+	hurricane	air filled with foam and spray; almost no visibility	major, widespread damage

PREDICTING WIND DIRECTION

Wind direction often follows a predictable sequence as fronts move through an area or the land warms and cools on a summer day. Knowing these patterns is useful for sea kayakers, since wind is often the most important factor that affects our travels.

The easiest wind to predict is the common sea breeze that develops on a warm, sunny day. The land heats up more quickly than the surrounding water, and the hot air above it

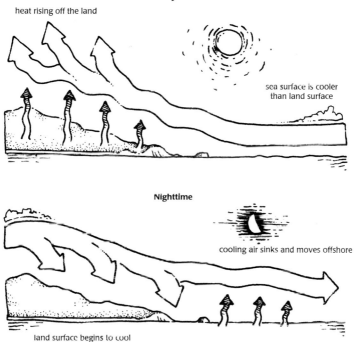

Daytime

heat rising off the land

sea surface is cooler than land surface

Nighttime

cooling air sinks and moves offshore

land surface begins to cool

One wind that is relatively easy to predict is the development of sea breezes on a warm, sunny day. These onshore winds can be quite strong by early afternoon. As the process reverses in the evening, a milder land breeze occurs.

rises. Cooler air from the water flows into this lower pressure area, creating a sea breeze blowing onshore. You can just about set your watch by this event on a typical summer day. Sea breezes begin to build by late morning and gain strength through the afternoon until the sun begins to wane and the process reverses itself. The land breeze created in the evening is usually far weaker than the sea breeze and blows offshore. If a weather system is moving through an area, sea breezes may be disrupted and less predictable.

Wind direction also follows a pattern related to the arrival and departure of weather fronts. Fronts are the boundaries between air masses of different temperature. In the Northern Hemisphere, when a cold front moves in to displace a warm front the wind will begin to *veer*, or move in a clockwise rotation. (In the Southern Hemisphere, the wind moves counterclockwise.) It will often move from the south to southwest as the cold front approaches and then continue to veer through the west, northwest, and finally north as the cold front passes. This generally brings cooler, drier air. However, the winds on the backside of a cold front can be strong and gusty, so you should be cautious about paddling in these conditions.

In the Northern Hemisphere, winds that shift in a counter-clockwise rotation are called *backing* winds. This is typically a shift from a southwesterly to south, southeast, and finally east. This backing wind will usually bring wetter weather that may linger until a cold front clears the air.

Knowing how weather front movements change the wind direction allows you to fine-tune your trip plans and make adjustments while under way. For example, knowing that the approach of a cold front is going to bring a veering wind that will result in strong winds out of the northwest (which happens to be offshore in your area) by early afternoon gives you the chance to change your plans. You could alter your route and paddle closer to shore, where there are plenty of bail-out points and better protection from these potentially dangerous conditions.

WEATHER SAYINGS AND OBSERVATIONS

One of the reasons that weather proverbs have lasted through the centuries is that many are more successful than the local meteorologist at predicting the weather! A proverb's scope might be more limited, but its words are often wise and easy to remember.

Sun dogs: Among the most commonly seen sky phenomena, these rainbow-colored halos appear on either or both sides of the sun. They indicate the presence of high-altitude cirrus clouds and usually predict a change in the weather.

Here are some favorites.

"Red sky at morning, sailor take warning; Red sky at night, sailor's delight."	A red sunset occurs because you are viewing the sun's rays through suspended dust particles. If the suspended dust is dry the sunset will appear red; if it is wet the sunset will appear as a yellowish or gray orb seen through a haze. Since most weather patterns in the temperate latitudes move from west to east, you are looking at tomorrow's weather. So a red sunset predicts fair and dry conditions for the following day. A red sunrise, on the other hand, occurs when the sun lights up the cirrus or cirrostratus clouds that have moved into an area, indicating the beginning of a weather pattern of lowering, thicker clouds that will usually turn wet over the course of the day or at least a pattern that will remain cloudy and unsettled.
"Dew In the night, next day will be bright."	If dew is present, you can expect fair weather. If the grass is dry, rain is on the way.
"Winds that swing against the sun and winds that bring the rain are one; Winds that swing around the sun keep the rainstorm on the run."	If the wind is moving from east to west, as the sun appears to, skies will usually be clear. If the winds shift from west to east, you can usually expect wetter weather. (This wind shift phenomenon can also be stated as "A backing wind says storms are nigh; but a veering wind will clear the sky." See pages 40–42 for more on predicting the wind direction.)
"When a halo rings the moon or sun, the rain will come upon the run."	A variety of weather sayings apply to halos, which also are useful predictors of weather. In general, a halo tells you there are clouds developing at high altitudes. The development of these cirrus and cirrostratus clouds is part of a pattern that usually brings rain.
"Mackerel sky and mare's tails make tall ships carry low sails."	A mackerel sky shows thickening cirrocumulus clouds, which are usually the precursors of wet, stormy weather.

Many more bits of weather lore are included in general observations that can help predict the weather like the direction of rising smoke from a campfire or chimney (rising smoke occurs during high pressure and fair weather; smoke that curls to the ground occurs during the low pressure of unsettled weather that usually brings rain). Smells are more pungent when there is moisture in the air as a warm front moves in.

WAVE HEIGHTS

Three factors determine wave size: the wind's velocity, the duration of time the wind blows from a given direction, and the fetch, or distance over which the wind blows unimpeded. Understanding these three factors allows you to make a rough estimate of what wave heights to expect when you're out on the water.

A stretch of coast that is wide open to the horizon and beyond (say, the Oregon coast) may have sizable waves crash on its shores when a strong wind has been blowing onshore for many hours. Maine, on the other hand, may not ever see any sizable seas along most of its midcoast shores where hundreds of islands disrupt the flow of wind.

When you're seated in the cockpit of your boat, even a small wave can look impressive. Your eye level is only about 26 to 30 inches off the surface of the water, so that towering wall of water descending on you may pack embarrassingly small statistics. This is not to say that 18-inch waves can't upset

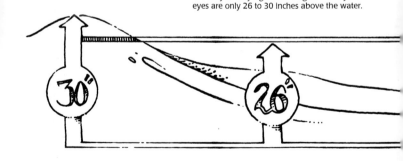

It's easy to misjudge wave heights when your eyes are only 26 to 30 inches above the water.

a kayak or make you pick your way cautiously through a crossing. A 30-inch wave is tall enough to block your view and make you lose sight of your paddling partners when you're sitting in its trough. But, beware of your wave height estimates. Just say they were "over your head" and let your listeners use their imaginations!

Wind Velocity, knots	Fetch, nm	Time, hours	Average Wave Height, ft.	Average of Highest 10%
10	10	2.4	0.9	1.8
15	34	6	2.5	5
20	75	10	5	10
25	160	16	9	18
30	280	23	14	28
50	1,420	69	48	99

Adapted from *Waves and Beaches*, by Willard Bascom

It takes a fairly potent combination of factors to build sizable seas. Knowing the three factors involved will help you understand and predict sea conditions.

GROUP TRAVEL

FORMATIONS

When a group of kayakers travels on the water, it may naturally tend to spread out or bunch up, with individuals traveling at a wide variety of paces. In the absence of boat traffic or challenging conditions, this might be fine. But most of the time, kayakers are faced with paddling in boat traffic, winds, or even fog or rough water.

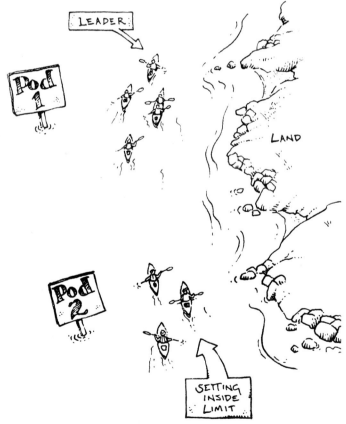

Larger groups may choose to break up into smaller pods. Pod leaders may set route limits along a shore or direct traffic during crossings.

Group members should paddle in an agreed-upon formation, maintaining visual contact at all times.

A group needs to travel in such a way that the weakest and strongest members are in visual contact at all times. Formations may differ based on group size, conditions, and the distances being traveled. For example, you may choose to appoint a lead boat and a sweep boat with other members captured between these two positions, or bracket the group on either side with leaders setting the inside and outside boundaries of travel. If the group is large, you might consider breaking into smaller pods with a leader in each. Pods may then travel in something like a diamond formation, where all members can see one another but remain with and have responsibilities to only a few other group members while on the water.

Groups will need to cross busy channels or shipping lanes quickly and in a compact formation to increase their visibility. One paddler may serve as "traffic cop" and use hand signals to send kayakers across or hold up group members until everyone is ready to cross. Other boaters will appreciate your courtesy.

Deciding on a group formation will require establishing group leaders. This is not to say that other paddlers in the group are passive participants. In fact, you may wish to swap leadership positions. The important thing is to make sure everyone understands their responsibilities and the signaling system that the group will use. Some positions in the group may fall naturally because of special talents or experience. Prior to leaving the launch site, group safety gear should be inventoried and all group members made aware of which paddler is carrying which pieces of equipment (towlines, repair kits, first-aid kits, and so on).

GROUP SIGNALS

Before setting out, all members of your group should agree on how they plan to communicate on the water. Voices can be difficult to hear and easy to misunderstand, so a system of whistle, hand, and paddle signals works best. These should be kept simple—no one needs to learn a new language at the beginning of every trip!

A small pealess whistle can be heard well on the water, but subtleties in pitch and the duration of blasts aren't that easy to detect, especially if you are in a stressful situation. Consider using a system like this:

- One blast to say "look at me." This is not used for emergency notice but simply to gain someone's attention.

- Two blasts to call someone back to the group. (The other paddler gives two blasts in return until visual contact is established.)

- If you need to use your whistle for an emergency signal, it is probably best to blow it repeatedly until you are noticed. There is little doubt that something is amiss when a whistle is being blown continuously. This is the best way to get the attention of other nearby boaters using a whistle (for distress signals, see pages 84–85).

Group members can also communicate by using hand or paddle signals. These are often easier to understand but require visual contact. Paddle signals are useful on the water or during surf landings. These same signals can be made using your hands. Here are some common ones:

stop

come ahead

go this way

CHALLENGES AT SEA

STRONG WINDS

Paddling in heavy winds (for most of us, anything above 15 knots) is challenging. You'll have to deal with the effect of the wind and with the seas it creates. Before setting out, be realistic about what it will take to travel under the conditions you're observing. You might be better off choosing another route or taking a windbound holiday.

Make sure your gear is secure on deck and the boat's load is well balanced; wind will accentuate the problems of a poorly trimmed boat. When you paddle in heavy winds, keep a low profile and use a lower-angle stroke that minimizes the windage of your paddle blades. If the wind is strong enough to lift the paddle from your hand, let go with your upwind hand and hold onto it with your downwind hand to retrieve it. You could well avoid a capsize by doing so.

Try to detect a rhythm to the wind; maintain your speed during gusts and paddle hard and make any corrective strokes during slack moments. Look around for any windbreaks, but be careful of using moored boats, since they may swing suddenly on their moorings. If you are faced with a long crossing, members of your group can swap positions and serve as windbreaks by letting others paddle in their lee (don't get so close that you risk a collision).

Try to set a cadence that you can maintain and look to the side to convince yourself you're really moving forward. Imagine breaking the distance into small segments and celebrate the completion of each segment. Staying upbeat is usually the hardest thing about paddling in heavy winds. Don't be

ON THE WATER

tempted to sprint or flail with your paddle; you'll waste invaluable energy. Stay loose through the hips as your boat pitches and rolls in any seas and try to keep your upper body still and relaxed. You may find that dropping a rudder or skeg is useful to keep you on course, though it may slow your progress.

BEAM SEAS

Beams seas come at you from the side, and if their timing is just right (and yours is terribly wrong), they can capsize you. Be ready to lean into the wave as it lifts the side of your boat and have your bracing skills on full alert. Avoid making a downwind stroke as the wave begins to lift your kayak—you could end up tripping over your paddle blade as your boat slides down the wave's face. Instead, make an upwind stroke as the boat is lifted; this will give you support and can correct your course if needed.

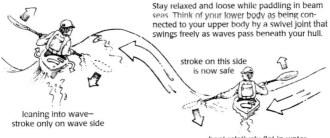

Stay relaxed and loose while paddling in beam seas. Think of your lower body as being connected to your upper body by a swivel joint that swings freely as waves pass beneath your hull.

stroke on this side is now safe

leaning into wave— stroke only on wave side

boat relatively flat in water

If the wind is coming off the bow quarter, you'll probably find that your kayak wants to turn into the wind, or weathercock. To correct this, lift the downwind edge of your boat and continue to paddle forward to keep the boat on course. You may occasionally have to throw in a forward sweep stroke on the upwind side to bring the boat back on course. To avoid losing forward momentum, make your corrections early and often. You can also drop a skeg or rudder; this creates drag at the stern and helps hold the boat on course, though it may slow your forward progress.

FOLLOWING SEAS

Paddling in following seas can range from the joys of a free ride to the unsettled feeling of being at the mercy of conditions you can't see sneaking up on you. Following seas will lift your stern and may make you feel unstable as the boat begins to gain speed down the face of the wave.

Here's a successful strategy for paddling in following seas:

- Make the most of the free ride portion by accelerating to catch the passing wave.

- Maintain a position perpendicular to the wave and continue to paddle forward when you get a helping hand.

- Once the crest has passed, continue to paddle forward but don't expend too much energy paddling up the backface of the wave.

- Try to sense a rhythm to the waves and develop a cadence that you can easily maintain.

There are two things you'll need to be careful of—pearling, or burying the bow of your boat in the water, and broaching, or getting turned sideways to the wave.

- To avoid pearling: Lean back to give your bow some lift and, if needed, back-paddle for a few strokes to let the wave pass beneath you.

- To avoid broaching: Make a quick corrective stroke as your boat is lifted to bring the boat perpendicular to the

surface movement

Develop a paddling pattern that takes advantage of the water's movement and try to keep your boat perpendicular to the waves. The best time to make corrections is at the crest of the wave when more of your boat is out of the water.

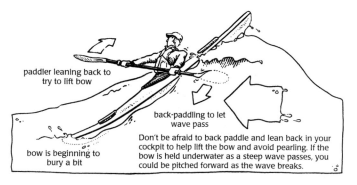

paddler leaning back to try to lift bow

back-paddling to let wave pass

bow is beginning to bury a bit

Don't be afraid to back paddle and lean back in your cockpit to help lift the bow and avoid pearling. If the bow is held underwater as a steep wave passes, you could be pitched forward as the wave breaks.

wave (this is the best timing since more of your boat is out of the water). Use a stern rudder stroke to regain position, though you will lose forward momentum. If you do get turned sideways, lean into the wave and brace on its crest until it passes beneath you and you can bring the boat back on course.

SQUALLS

The only good news about squalls is that they are short-lived—but their rapid passing can be violent and dangerous. A squall line often forms on the front edge of a strong cold front and can be seen as a line of low-lying dark and ominous clouds. Often these represent a line of classic thunderheads. At other times they are seen as a rolling, boiling line of stratocumulus and nimbus clouds. Because a squall precedes a strong cold front, the winds will suddenly begin to shift to the

south and then southwest as the squall approaches. Barometric pressure drops suddenly (though by that point the squall line should be easily visible). A squall line brings strong and gusty winds and is usually accompanied by pelting rain that can thicken and even blow sideways and obscure visibility. Lightning and hail may accompany a squall line.

In general, a squall line seen to the south or southeast of your position will pass you by; a squall line to the north or northwest of your position may well be headed your way.

React quickly to the approach of a squall line. If possible, get off the water and secure the boats. If you're caught on open water, you will not be able to outrun the squall; look for something to duck behind for protection. If there's no protection available, point into the wind and keep a steady cadence with a low-angle stroke; be ready to brace in any sudden wind gusts. (For a discussion of lightning, see page 85.)

After a squall line passes, the wind may continue to shift to the west and then north, with skies clearing and cooler, and drier weather moving into the area.

FOG

Fog can humble the best of navigators and rattle the most confident among us. It can distort sounds, wipe out all references to landmarks, and leave you feeling completely disoriented. Although fog can move in quickly, you will see it approaching. If fog is moving into your area try to head for a known location and begin taking bearings to known objects until visibility is lost or you reach land. Continue to hug known shorelines or simply take a break from paddling and go ashore until the conditions improve.

If you are disoriented in the fog, first sit very still and listen for water lapping against rocks, which will indicate a nearby shoreline, or other identifiable sound (road, airport). If you see a place to land, paddle to it even if you are unsure of where you are. If you cannot see any land, point your bow into the wind and try to get oriented using your chart and your last known position.

Watch the movement of the water. Can you observe any tidal current? Couple your knowledge of the times for low and high water with your observations of the tidal current to gain

You'll need to keep your senses finely tuned when paddling in fog. Avoid crossings, exposed stretches of water, and high boat traffic areas If at all possible.

a general orientation. For example, If you know you are observing an ebbing tide and you are pointed into a tidal current, you know you must be pointed toward the area from which the tide is ebbing. Now refer to your chart and begin to narrow down your possible locations. Can you see any bottom features that match your chart? Gather as many pieces of the puzzle as you can using your observations, chart, compass, and tide table until you gain a better picture of your location.

When you navigate in fog, you need to be cautious. If you must make a crossing, do so by overcorrecting for the tidal current so any shoreline you hit is clearly above or below your intended point and you can paddle to your destination along a piece of land. Always have your foghorn and whistle handy to give notice of your location if another vessel approaches your position.

BOAT TRAFFIC

Rather than quote from Rules of the Road (the body of law that covers the conduct and requirements of all vessels on all waters), we should look at commonsense approaches to paddling in congested waters. Kayaks are incredibly versatile craft; we have the ability to stop on a dime and back-paddle, and we can tuck up into places where no other vessel would dare go.

We are small and quick, but we are also very difficult to see, especially for large vessels. We don't show up on radar on a reliable basis, and our firepower of signaling devices is often woefully inadequate. So we must do everything we can to be seen and to make predictable moves.

Shipping channels and other deep-water channels are marked on navigational charts and are readily discernible when you're on the water. Larger boats have to stay inside the boundaries of these marked channels or risk running aground. Kayakers can usually stay just outside these channels and avoid interfering with boat traffic—kind of like walking on the

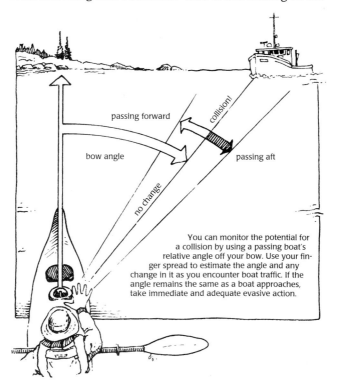

passing forward

collision!

bow angle

passing aft

no change

You can monitor the potential for a collision by using a passing boat's relative angle off your bow. Use your finger spread to estimate the angle and any change in it as you encounter boat traffic. If the angle remains the same as a boat approaches, take immediate and adequate evasive action.

sidewalk while traffic whizzes by on a busy road. If you're in doubt about who has the right of way, be sensible. It is almost always easier for you to yield.

If you must cross a channel, do so quickly and at a right angle to the channel. Wait for a break in traffic and dart across, keeping everyone in the group clustered together. This is no place for sightseeing or pausing for a group picture. Beware of wakes from passing vessels; even in wake-restricted zones these can pile up and be a challenge to kayakers.

Keep a wary eye out for boats on moorings or even tied to docks. They may suddenly swing on their lines or shift with a gust of wind or wake from a passing vessel. Stay well away from any vessels that are being controlled by tugs. If you see a tug and barge on open water, you must assume they are connected even if you can't see the hawser. Never paddle between two such vessels. Boats under sail may need to make adjustments to the wind that require crossing your path, and fishing vessels such as lobster boats and draggers have set courses determined by their gear placement. Anticipate the needs of other vessels and understand their limitations as well as your own.

To judge whether or not you are on a collision course with another vessel, maintain a steady course (compass or landmark) and note whether an approaching vessel's course has changed relative to its angle off your bow. If there is no change, you are on a collision course and must take an evasive action. Legalities are of less concern than survival.

In busy harbors it is usually best to stay just outside boat traffic lanes. You'll often need 360-degree vision as you pick your way through traffic. Be particularly wary of boats backing out of slipways or pulling away from docks.

NIGHT PADDLING

TRAVELING SAFELY

Night paddlers need to make sure everyone in the group understands the need to stay close and within voice contact of each other. You might consider marking each paddler or boat with Cyalume sticks and make sure everyone has a white light readily available.

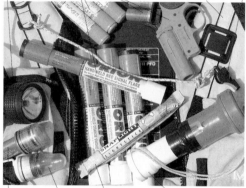

headlamp   various types of flares   reflective tape   whistle

flashlight   strobe light   light stick   manual horn

If your life vest does not have retroreflective tape along the shoulders and upper back, add some. At night these highly visible strips of material are easy to pick out with just a flash of light in their general direction. You should also add this reflective tape to your boat. All night paddlers should also carry whistles, aerial flares, and a strobe light on the back shoulder of their life vest.

You will need a small light mounted on your compass. For chart reading, a red lens on a penlight will give you sufficient illumination but won't interfere with your night vision. Include numerous breaks for regrouping and consider instituting the buddy system while under way. Navigating at night in unknown waters is not recommended for inexperienced kayakers.

NIGHT SIGNALS

At night, your signaling equipment will be somewhat more limited than the array available to you during the day. Human-powered vessels are required to carry a white light that can be exhibited in time to prevent a collision. Kayaks are not required to show running lights of any kind, though it may be prudent to use a white light under the deck rigging or a headlamp while under way in boat traffic. If for any reason you were stopped in the water for a period of time, mark your position with a white light. You should also note the presence of any navigational aids with light characteristics along your route.

At night your distress signals may be limited to red aerial flares, a continuously sounded foghorn, an EPIRB (emergency position-indicating radio beacon), and a Mayday call over your VHF radio. Rules for Inland Waters also recognize a white flashing strobe as an emergency signal. These emergency strobes are useful for kayakers. They show up well at night and can be attached to the boat or to the life vest on the back shoulder, where they can be seen if you are floating in the water.

If you regularly paddle at night in areas with other boat traffic, especially commercial traffic, you should learn the running and anchor lights for other vessels. The color, number, and placement of these lights will tell you the size and type of vessel and whether it is moving or stationary. This is invaluable at night, since it may be hard to discern that two vessels are connected (tug and barge) or whether a vessel is approaching or moving away from your position. Both the COLREGS and Unified Rules (available from marine chandleries) list the light requirements for all vessels under way and at anchor.

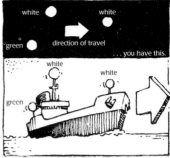

If you see this at night . . .
white   white
green   direction of travel
. . . you have this.

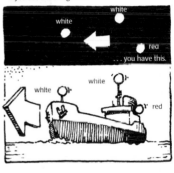

If you see this at night . . .
white
white
red
. . . you have this.

If the two white lights are aligned . . .
white
white
green   red
. . . you'd better get out of the way!

Night paddlers need to become familiar with the running and anchor lights of vessels plying the local waters. Sometimes these lights are the only way to determine a vessel's position and direction of travel.

Navigation

NAVIGATION SKILLS

COMPASS ROSE

The compass rose is a convenient feature on navigational charts that allows you to take bearings directly off the chart without having to orient the chart or use a protractor. The compass rose is really three rings of compass directions. The outer ring gives "true" directions that have not been corrected for variation (called declination on topographic maps). Thus, true north lies at the top of the chart. Variation is the difference between true north and magnetic north. The variation for a given area can be found at the center of the compass rose and may vary slightly from one compass rose to the next on the same chart. The change in variation over time is also given, though this is insignificant for our purposes.

The middle ring of the compass rose is the one kayakers use. Directions are given as magnetic bearings, which is what your compass will read when you are under way. Using the middle ring of the compass rose prevents your having to make any corrections. Instead, there is (or should be) direct agreement between your compass and what you read from the middle ring of the compass rose.

The inner ring of the compass rose is also oriented magnetically and harks back to the days when compass directions were given as points rather than degrees. Compass points mark the cardinal (e.g., north) and intercardinal (e.g., northeast) directions as well as those between for a total of 32 points. Each compass point is 11.25 degrees.

When you are folding your chart to fit into your chartcase, try to include a compass rose so you can see it at a glance. If that's not possible, take the magnetic cardinal and intercardinal directions and transfer them so you will have some reference (i.e., N, NE, E, SE, S, SW, W, NW) when you glance at the folded chart.

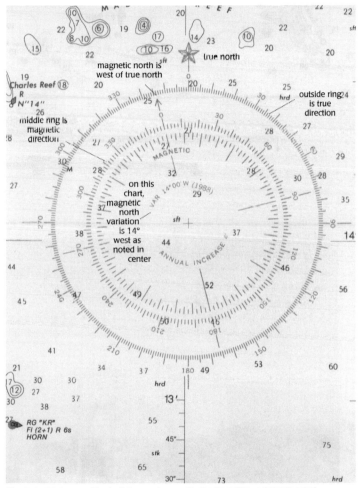

The compass rose provides both true and magnetic directions. The variation is noted and can change across a single chart. Since kayakers only cover small distances in a given day, we may use magnetic directions and read directly from our compass.

BUOYS

Buoys are invaluable signposts on the water because they tell you with reasonable accuracy where you are. Buoys float in the water and are anchored to the bottom. They are distinguished by their color, shape, and number and the presence of any sound or light signals. There is a system to their placement in a waterway that can be determined from their color and number. More than 25,000 buoys are maintained in U.S. waters alone.

Buoys may be cylindrical (called *cans*) or a cylinder topped with a cone (called *nuns*). These two shapes are easy to distinguish even when they are backlit and you can't discern colors. Nuns are painted red and cans are green, though there are buoys that use horizontal or vertical striping of two colors to mark channel junctions (red and green horizontal) and safe water approaches (red and white vertical), respectively. Odd numbers are used on cans and mark the port (left) side of a channel leading in from seaward; nun buoys are even numbered and mark the starboard (right) side of the channel leading in from seaward. Numbers increase from seaward on all buoys. (Note: In many areas, "returning from seaward" is a rather ambiguous direction.)

Buoys are clearly marked on charts: RN for red nun and GC for green can. Their numbers are shown in quotation marks to distinguish them from the numbers used for soundings.

Some buoys may show letters when marking offshore hazards. For example, the buoy "4HL" is a red nun buoy that marks Halibut Ledge. Buoys may carry a variety of lights and sound

green can buoy is cylindrical and always bears an odd number

red nun buoy is conical and always bears an even number

signals and may have both sound and light characteristics. In general, the greater the marquee value of a buoy, the more notice of it is needed. For example, a large red buoy with a gong and flashing light might mark an important entrance from seaward that no vessel wants to miss.

daybeacon

You may also encounter daybeacons, which are affixed to ledges, rocks, or structures onshore or in shallow water. They are typically used to mark channels and hazards and their system of identification corresponds to buoys. Triangular daybeacons are red and bordered by red reflective material, and numbers will be even; square daybeacons are green and bordered by green reflective material, and their numbers will be odd. Daybeacons may also carry lights to help mark a channel and may use horizontal or vertical striping in a manner similar to can and nun buoys.

The United States adheres to the IALA (International Association of Lighthouse Authorities) B system (red to starboard) of buoyage, as do the rest of North America, South America, Japan, Korea, and the Philippines. The remainder of the world uses the A system (red to port). Other buoyage systems or special markings may be used for inland waters, the intracoastal waterway, private moorings, or other special circumstances.

GC "3"   RN "6"   Bn

can buoy   nun buoy   daybeacon

Buoys have their own language and provide a great deal of information through their color, shape, number, size, and the presence of light and sound signals. The representations to the left are examples of how they appear on a nautical chart. See NOAA *Chart No. 1* for full details.

LIGHT CHARACTERISTICS

Lighthouses and buoys may be given specific light characteristics and are important aids to navigation. Many lighthouses are prominent displays whose lights will be the first
thing seen when approaching land from offshore. Light characteristics are defined by their color (red, green, or white) and
their rhythm. These light characteristics will be marked on a
chart adjacent to the designation for a lighted buoy or lighthouse. A lighthouse is marked by a magenta exclamation
point, a lighted buoy by a magenta dot at the base of the buoy
marker.

Navigating at night is not recommended for inexperienced
kayakers. But the possibility of poor visibility during daytime
paddling means *every* paddler must able to identify lighted
navigational aids. It can also be fun to sit on an island shore at
the end of the day and identify the lights you find on your
chart. The light pattern or rhythm is made by varying the intervals of light and darkness. Here are some of the most common
light rhythms and their notations on a chart:

Light Phase Characteristics

Light Pattern	Abbreviations and Meanings		Phase Description
	Lights That Don't Change Color	Lights That Show Color Variations	
	F. = Fixed	Alt. = Alternating	a continuous steady light
	F. Fl. = Fixed and flashing	Alt. F. Fl. = Alternating fixed and flashing	a fixed light varied at regular intervals by a flash of greater brilliance
	F. Gp. Fl. = Fixed and group and flashing	Alt. F. Gp. Fl. = Alternating fixed and group flashing	a fixed light varied at regular intervals by groups of 2 or more flashes of greater brilliance
	Fl. = Flashing	Alt. Fl. = Alternating flashing	showing a single flash at regular intervals, the duration of light always being less than the duration of darkness
	Gp. Fl. = Group flashing	Alt. Gp. Fl. = Alternating group flashing	showing at regular intervals groups of 2 or more flashes
	Gp. Fl. (1 + 2) = Composite group flashing	—	light flashes are combined in alternate groups of different numbers
	E. Int. = Equal interval	—	light with all durations of light and darkness equal
	Occ. = Occulting	Alt. Occ. = Alternating occulting	a light totally eclipsed at regular intervals, the duration of light always greater than the duration of darkness
	Gp. Occ. = Group occulting	—	a light with a group of 2 or more eclipses at regular intervals
	Gp. Occ. (2 + 3) = Composite group occulting	—	a light in which the occultations are combined in alternate groups of different numbers

Lights on navigation aids can be identified by their color and light rhythm. Varying the light and dark intervals produces distinctive patterns that may identify a particular light. One full cycle of changes is the light's period.

LATITUDE-LONGITUDE READINGS

Imagine the globe with an invisible grid laid over its surface. The grid would allow you to give the address of a location as the intersection of these lines, expressed in degrees and minutes (one degree equals 60 minutes, and one minute equals 60 seconds). Latitude tells you how far it is north or south of the equator. Longitude tells you how far it is east or west of the Greenwich meridian. For example, a favorite paddling spot might be: latitude 44 degrees 1 minute north and longitude 69 degrees 4 minutes west. You can mark this as an exact location on a chart, plug it into a GPS (global positioning system) receiver, or radio it to the coast guard in the event of an emergency.

Latitude-longitude readings are the most precise way of pinpointing locations on the globe. However, kayakers rarely make use of actual latitude-longitude readings for locations. We tend to use common names or combinations of names and compass directions, since we are generally paddling where there are numerous landmarks. You might find you use latitude-longitude readings more if you utilize a GPS, which spits them out like ticker tape while under way. (For more on using a GPS, see pages 80–81.)

The distance between two consecutive lines of latitude is equal anywhere you go on earth. One degree of latitude is 60 nautical miles, and thus one minute of latitude is one nautical mile.

A nautical mile is slightly longer than a statute mile, which is commonly used on land and is 5,280 feet. Using nautical miles is best for navigating, since we can use the latitude lines on a chart for a quick measure of distance rather than relying on the chart scale, which might be hidden within a folded chart.

Note that while you can use latitude lines for measuring distances, you cannot do the same with longitude lines; longitude lines converge at the poles and the distance between any two consecutive longitude lines changes as you approach them.

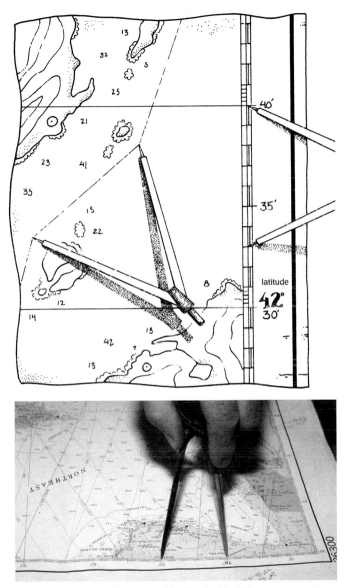

You can use the latitude scale along the side of the chart for distance measurements. One minute of latitude is equal to one nautical mile. Five-minute latitude lines are often printed across the entire chart and can be handy for quick reference when the full scale is folded under in a chartcase.

TAKING A BEARING

A bearing is simply a direction to some landmark. You may take a bearing while under way by pointing your bow at an object, like a buoy, and reading your deck compass. Or, you may mark bearings on your chart from one object to another for reference (say, from one island to another island). A bearing may define your course, or the direction you want to go, but it is not necessarily your compass course or your heading, which is the direction your boat is pointed. A bearing simply gives you a direction to an object.

It is useful to note a variety of bearings during the trip-planning phase. You can mark these on the surface of your chartcase with a grease pencil or record them on note cards that you keep inside your chartcase. Take your bearings over short distances and from obvious objects or land features whenever possible (and note your back bearing, or return, which is sim-

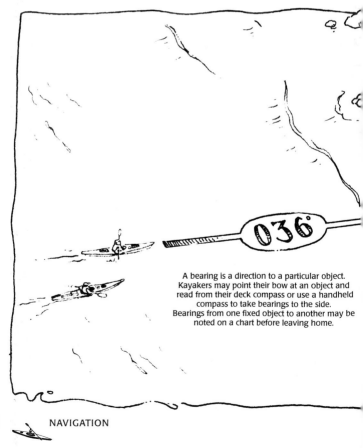

A bearing is a direction to a particular object. Kayakers may point their bow at an object and read from their deck compass or use a handheld compass to take bearings to the side. Bearings from one fixed object to another may be noted on a chart before leaving home.

ply 180 degrees from your original bearing). Note that using bearings to and from buoys prior to setting out can be a problem; a buoy's location on a chart is not particularly accurate, since it may be moved or dragged by currents.

To take bearings while under way, point your bow at an object and read your deck compass. If you don't want to swing your bow around to point directly at an object, you can use a handheld compass. Always note your bearings as a series of three numbers; if you yell to your paddling partner that the lighthouse is at a bearing of "36," she might wonder if she didn't hear a "1" or a "2" in front of the "36" or a "0" at the end. Be sure to say "zero," which is clearer than "oh," for a zero. Remember that you're reading from your deck compass and the middle ring of the compass rose, so your bearings are always magnetic. This could be critical if you have to make an emergency call and give your location in relation to something.

LINE OF POSITION

A line of position will not pinpoint your location, but it will narrow your choices by placing you somewhere along a particular line of travel. Say you can sight a tower over the bow of your kayak. By lining up your deck compass with the tower, you read a magnetic bearing of 112 degrees. If you were in a pilothouse of a large vessel and had your chart spread across a table, you could use a set of parallel rules to draw a line at 112 degrees magnetic (or 292 degrees magnetic as the back bearing) that ended (or started, for the back bearing) at the tower. You know you would be somewhere along the line you have drawn. This is your line of position at that moment in time. You would label this line with the bearing and the time the bearing was taken.

Kayakers don't have the luxury of spreading charts across a flat surface and using parallel rules while under way. But you can roughly estimate the correct line with the edge of your hand, sliding it parallel from your compass rose. Or better still, use a small courser or grid ruler that you can quickly overlay and that will allow you to mark a line of correct orientation. Use a grease pencil to mark on the surface of your chartcase. This may not seem a highly refined way to navigate, but it works quite well for our purposes.

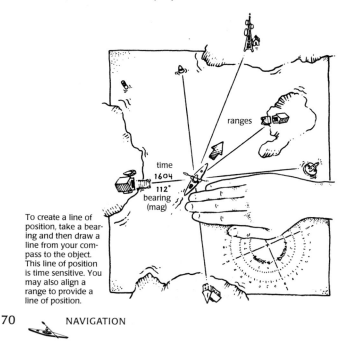

ranges

time
1604

112°
bearing
(mag)

To create a line of position, take a bearing and then draw a line from your compass to the object. This line of position is time sensitive. You may also align a range to provide a line of position.

RANGES

A range is an alignment of any two objects that is used to determine a line of position. Ranges can be natural or navigational. Kayakers can utilize a variety of ranges over the course of a day's paddling, discarding them along the way. Some ranges might already be marked on your chart; large vessels use these to find their way along a stretch of river or through a dredged channel to safe harbor. Think twice about utilizing these ranges, since they will put you into a channel with large boat traffic.

Instead, pick two stationary objects, one behind the other, along your line of travel (say, a smokestack and a large, distinctive rock). If you continue to keep these two objects aligned, you are on course; if they no longer appear aligned, you know you have drifted off course. If the farthest object in your range drifts to the right of the closer object, you are to the right of your course. Move your boat to the left until the objects realign. If the farthest object is to the left of the nearest object, move right to bring them back in line.

Ranges are invaluable for the feedback they give you about conditions that may set you off your course. Unlike paddling toward a single object, using a range will keep you on a particular course and let you know when you have strayed from it. It is often easier to paddle utilizing a range than monitoring a deck compass.

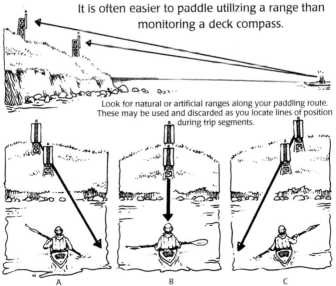

Look for natural or artificial ranges along your paddling route. These may be used and discarded as you locate lines of position during trip segments.

| A | B | C |

If the two objects in the range are not aligned you will need to make adjustments to get back on course. In (A), the paddler needs to move to the right to bring the range into alignment. In (C), the paddler needs to move to the left.

DETERMINING SPEED OF TRAVEL

You need to know how fast you are moving to know when you can expect to arrive at your destination. In perfectly calm conditions where there is no wind or current, your paddling speed is all you need to determine. Most touring kayakers travel at speeds between 2 and 4 knots (nautical miles per hour) over a day of paddling. This is not to say that you can't kick your paddling into overdrive to reach a sprint speed of 5.5 knots, but you won't maintain this over a day of travel.

With experience, you can get a handle on your own paddling speed. You'll know you can count on maintaining a pace of, say, 2.5 knots through all but the most demanding conditions. You know what it feels like to maintain this pace and can detect when it has become a hard slog or an easy ride. But it would be nice to get a more quantitative handle on this matter.

Choose a calm day at slack water and paddle a pre-measured nautical mile that is marked on your chart. Pick a pace that you know will be a comfortable touring pace and time yourself over this course several times. Or, paddle between any two measurable points in protected waters and calculate your speed in knots (nautical miles per hour).

Knowing your normal speed in the absence of wind and currents will allow you to more accurately determine your speed made good, or your net speed under real conditions. For example, if you know that your paddling speed is normally 2.5 knots, you would expect to make a one-mile crossing in 0.4 hours, or 24 minutes. Instead, you found that it took a full hour for you to make the crossing; your speed made good was actually 1.0 knot. So the actual conditions of wind and current affected your speed by 1.5 knots. This is important information to store away for future reference.

If you know the strength of a tidal current in advance, you can calculate what to expect for a speed made good before setting out. If you knew from your tidal current tables that you would be bucking a current of 1.5 knots, you would expect your speed made good to be 1.0 knot, or the difference between your average paddling speed (2.5 knots) and the speed of the current (1.5 knots). You would then take this piece of information into account in your trip planning.

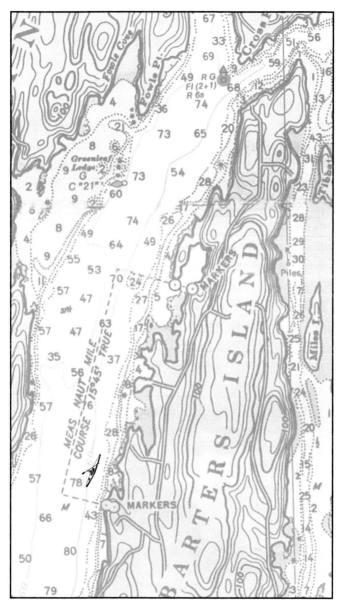

Find your paddling speed by utilizing a measured course marked on your chart, or lay one out in your paddling area. Knowing your typical cruising speed will come in handy when planning a trip and to monitor your progress during your trip.

DETERMINING A FIXED POINT

Getting a fix on your position is reassuring, and you can use it to determine the effects of wind and tidal current or to mark your progress. You can do this by noting your location at an identifiable object, such as a buoy, or you can determine it using two or more lines of position.

First, record your line of position (see page 70) and mark it on your chart, noting the bearing and time. Now, take a bearing to another object, preferably at a right angle to the original bearing. Draw a line of position from this bearing. You are theoretically at the point where these two lines intersect; you have a "fix" on your position. There is a degree of uncertainty, but this refines your location significantly. You will minimize the error in this method if you keep your lines of position at right angles.

You can continue to obtain additional lines of position for reassurance and to bracket your position. This is useful if you have doubts about the intersection of your original two lines of position. Try to take all your bearings as quickly as possible so the boat will not have changed position. Remember to be consistent about utilizing the middle ring of the compass rose for magnetic bearings.

Marine compasses are different from compasses meant to be used on land. A marine compass has the bearing numbers printed on a plate that rotates to maintain its northerly orientation. It can be attached to the deck of a kayak without adjusting it. It's read by viewing the bearing as indicated at the lubber line (a fixed line on the compass aligned with the boat's longitudinal axis). Marine charts show the magnetic variation on the compass rose, so you can navigate using only magnetic directions.

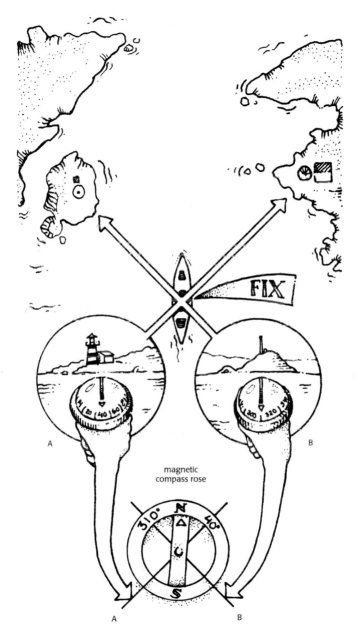

A fix can be determined from the intersection of different lines of position. Try and get two lines of position at right angles to one another for the best accuracy.

TIDAL CURRENT CALCULATIONS

Tidal current can affect both your travel speed and your course. If the current is in line with your course, only your speed of travel will be affected. If the current is at any angle to your course, it will set you off course.

You may find the speed and time of the tidal current by referring to the *Tidal Current Tables* compiled by the National Ocean Service or to a tidal current chart of your area. You can also determine the current while under way by timing your drift over a known distance. Using this information you can determine what to expect for your speed made good. One handy and quick way to do this is to note the time it takes for the length of your boat to drift past a stationary point. You can use this for a quick calculation of the speed of the tidal current. For example, if your 17-foot boat takes 5 seconds to drift past a piling, the current is moving at 17 feet per 5 seconds. Now convert this into knots—(17 feet/5 seconds) x (1 nautical mile/6,076 feet) x (3,600 seconds/hour)—and you see that you have drifted at 2.0 knots:

$$\frac{17 \text{ ft.}}{5 \text{ sec.}} \times \left(\frac{1 \text{ nm}}{6076 \text{ ft.}}\right) \times \left(\frac{3600 \text{ sec.}}{1 \text{ hour}}\right) = \frac{2 \text{ nm (knots)}}{\text{hour}}$$

You can do the same calculation by observing the drift of an object, such as a piece of seaweed, as it passes your stationary boat (hold onto the piling). The important point to remember is that, in a 17-foot boat, 5 seconds is 2.0 knots.

If the tidal current is running at a right angle to your course

Knowing that a 17-foot boat that drifts past a point in 5 seconds is moving at 2.0 knots is a handy reference. You can use this to estimate tidal current or even your own cruising speed while under way.

(typical in a channel crossing), you will have to determine how much it will set you off course. The easiest way to do this is to divide the speed of the current by your paddling speed and multiply this by the distance of your crossing. This will tell you how far down you can expect to be set by the tidal current in this channel. For example, if you are paddling a crossing of one nautical mile and you know from past experience or a tidal current table that the current in this crossing at this time is 1.5 knots and that you normally paddle at 2.5 knots, you can calculate that

1.5 knots (current speed) ÷ 2.5 knots (paddling speed)
x 1 nautical mile (crossing distance) = 0.6 nautical miles
(distance you will be set over by the current)

Obviously, the result of this calculation is significant. If you plan on crossing this channel you will either need to accept the extra 0.6-mile slog against the current to get to your desired location or point up into the current to a spot 0.6 miles above your intended destination and ferry across the channel.

These calculations are not exact, but they are useful for kayakers. The strength of the tidal current is not equal throughout the crossing but will probably reach its maximum in the deep water at the center of the channel. You might consider paddling slightly over 0.6 miles into the current along the edge of the channel before making your crossing. This would more than offset the effect of the tidal current and should result in your reaching the far shore slightly above your destination for an easy float into your landing. This is sometimes called an "up-and-over" crossing.

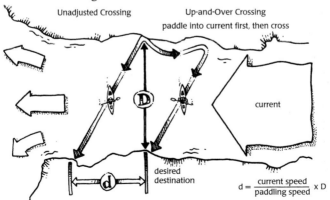

You can calculate the distance of the tidal set if you know the speed of the tidal current and your paddling speed. Though these factors are assumed to be constant in calculations, you can still use this simple equation to help with trip planning and paddling strategy.

WHERE AM I?

Feeling lost on the water is a gut-wrenching feeling, but rarely is it more than a momentary disorientation for touring kayakers. If you're exploring new areas, you may find it difficult to match the bird's-eye view on your chart with what you observe from your cockpit. A cluster of islands can look like a continuous piece of shoreline, and a change in tidal level can create entirely new landscapes.

Get used to repeatedly looking behind you as you paddle away from a shoreline, and try to fix in your mind landmarks and the general lay of the land for future reference. Noting features such as an unusual rock formation or a brightly colored house may come in handy for reorienting yourself.

If you're not sure where you are, first try to maintain a position, preferably by pulling onto a piece of nearby shoreline. Look for buoys or daybeacons that you can then find on your chart to pinpoint your position. Try to match the contour of nearby islands or mainland shoreline to an area on your chart. Where is your position in relation to the sun, wind direction, and tidal current direction? Pointing your kayak toward the sun or with a tidal flow can help you reorient by narrowing your view to one direction (say, west in the afternoon as you point into the sun). Now try to identify landmarks that lie in that general direction.

Before you launch it's also helpful to note a direction that will return you to a mainland shore. For instance, in Maine you can aim in a northwesterly direction and be fairly confident you're at least heading toward a mainland shore instead of out to sea, since the coast of Maine lies generally along a southwest–northeast axis. Off the southern coast of Alaska, you would do well to paddle in a northerly direction to hit a mainland shore. This is not an exact return bearing (or *back azimuth*) that you recorded as you launched, but a general sense of where your mainland shore can be found.

Getting reoriented is like solving a puzzle. Use each observation you make to narrow your choices of where you are until the pieces fall into place and you can find your location on the chart (see pages 54–55 for tips on paddling in fog).

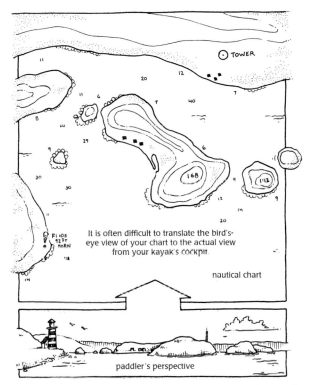

It is often difficult to translate the bird's-eye view of your chart to the actual view from your kayak's cockpit.

nautical chart

paddler's perspective

Islands that look clearly separated on your chart will often look like one long coastline when viewed from your cockpit. You may need to take bearings to identify them.

contour interval

paddler's perspective

As you look at land masses on the chart, you'll need to imagine their actual height and shape (think of pulling the tops of the hills up like a Slinky toy, with each ring being a contour line).

200
50

chart representation

+ 307

+ 360

ELECTRONIC NAVIGATION

GPS WAYPOINTS

Over the past several years, GPS (global positioning system) receivers have gotten less expensive and more accurate. Rugged waterproof models are handy tools for sea kayakers and other outdoor enthusiasts, but they shouldn't replace a thorough understanding of land or sea navigation. Anything electronic is likely to fail at some point, so total reliance on this instrument is not smart.

A GPS notes your position in relation to a variety of small satellites that are able to triangulate to within an impressively small window of uncertainty. You can record waypoints (exact latitude and longitude locations) while under way or store them in advance. A GPS will also give the bearing to a waypoint from your position and record your speed of travel.

To utilize a GPS you should first understand latitude and longitude and how to read these from a nautical chart (see pages 66–67). You can load hundreds of these locations into your GPS as waypoints that you can use for navigation. It is comforting to know you have loaded waypoints in advance when the visibility decreases to a boat length or two. Recording waypoints while under way will provide you with reference points for your return leg or mark an exact spot, like a good fishing hole, for future reference.

As you paddle toward a waypoint, the GPS screen will show your path and the bearing you need to get there (you

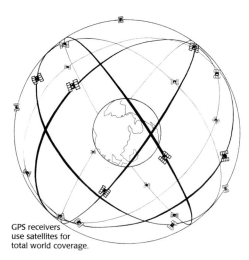

GPS receivers use satellites for total world coverage.

can usually choose between true and magnetic bearings). Don't forget to continue recording all the bearings and your lines of position the old fashioned way, since a suddenly blank screen is a real possibility.

STORING GPS INFORMATION

Even though most GPS units have impressive memories, you'll probably find that you'll need to organize the information you have stored in them. Beware of letting the GPS continue to run while under way and recording waypoints every several minutes—this uses up valuable storage capacity and most likely will need to be cleared before the next trip.

The most difficult thing about storing a large number of waypoints is finding one again without scrolling through a long list of candidates. In the absence of tagging the waypoint with a name (usually only four or five characters is allowed), most GPS units simply number them in the order they were added. It is worth taking some time to decide how you will use your GPS and how you need to store and access information—particularly if your GPS unit doesn't have a "find" command. Develop a consistent and simple naming process. Many GPS units can show a list of waypoints in order of their distance from your present location. This is a handy feature, since you can view waypoints in relation to your position rather than scroll through a long alphabetical or numbered list.

A GPS unit can store an amazing amount of data for retrieval while under way. You still need a chart and a deck or handheld compass as backup in case of electronic meltdown.

ON THE AIR

VHF RADIO SIGNALS

VHF stands for "very high frequency" and is a common radio signal used by vessels for communication. VHF radio signals carry over a distance that is slightly more than line of sight and can be affected by strong weather and the signal's own source of power. These signals can carry invaluable safety communications as well as links to mainland communication lines.

VHF radios transmit over an area slightly longer than line of sight. When using a hand-held unit, you'll often need to pick an open piece of water or a high spot on an island to get good reception and transmission.

Particular VHF channels are used for specific purposes, and there are operating rules for use of a VHF radio. These rules have been established to keep certain channels open for distress calls (channel 16) only and reduce channel overcrowding.

Become familiar with local preferences in radio channels. Local fishermen, marinas, and other services will favor specific channels for their communications. Check with a local harbormaster, marine chandlery, or paddlesports shop to find out the VHF channel preferences for the area where you plan to paddle. Unless you're using another channel for communication, your radio should be set on channel 16, the distress and safety frequency.

VHF RADIO PROTOCOL

You must have a license and register your station name and assigned call letters with the FCC before using a VHF radio. At a minimum, you must identify your station and its call letters at the beginning and the end of an exchange of transmissions with another station. It is helpful to use the term "over" at the end of each individual transmission so the receiver knows you are awaiting a response. When you transmit, you will be unable to hear transmissions from others, so brevity is preferred.

If you wish to call another boat or the marine operator, ac-

VHF DISTRESS CALLS ON CHANNEL 16

The three levels of priority for channel 16 messages are

- Sécurité (pronounced *say-KYUR-e-tay*): safety announcements. For example, alerting other boats to your presence in foggy conditions. The coast guard may use this message priority to announce buoy changes.

- Pan-Pan (pronounced *pahn-pahn*): urgent message priority. For example, a kayak guide sending an alert about a lost paddler or coast guard announcing a received distress call to boaters in the area.

- Mayday: highest priority signal given when someone is in danger of death. All boaters in the area must respond to these calls if at all possible.

These messages should be announced by repeating the message priority three times (e.g., Pan-Pan, Pan-Pan, Pan-Pan), citing your call sign, noting your position (if applicable), and then making your announcement.

cess the proper channel and then say the name of whom you wish to contact followed by "this is" and your station name and call letters. (For example: "Fishing vessel *Bobbie-Sue*, this is small craft *Sea Cat*, AABB, over.") You may retransmit this request up to three times, at least two minutes apart. If you do not get a response, you must wait at least fifteen minutes before trying again. When you wish to contact someone, you should transmit only the above information so that the call lasts only about thirty seconds.

If you receive a call on your VHF radio, acknowledge the call with the name of the boat that is calling and then say, "this is" and give your station name and call sign. Always end each transmission with the word "over." The other party will name a channel to move to for continuing the communication. When communications are completed, state "this is," give your station name and call sign, and then say "out."

Adhering to VHF radio protocol is important because it gives messages "right of way" based on their urgency and keeps the flow of everyday communications smooth and understandable.

Emergency Situations

WHEN THINGS GO WRONG

DISTRESS SIGNALS

Certain types of signaling devices are defined as distress signals under both international and U.S. jurisdiction. To utilize this equipment is to say you need help; your signal must be reported and, if possible, answered by any nearby vessels. In other words, the use of distress signals is not to be taken lightly.

Distress signals that are officially recognized on both international and inland waters and that are feasible for kayakers include: dye markers, smoke signals, red aerial flares (pencil, meteor, or parachute), a continuously sounded foghorn, an EPIRB (emergency position-indicating radio beacon), waving

red meteor flares

parachute red flare

Aerial flares: check expiration dates before heading out. Pencil flares are relatively inexpensive and fit in life vest pocket (but not as powerful as meteor or parachute flares).

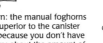

Smoke (left) and dye markers (right): store these in a dry container when not paddling.

foghorn sounded continuously

Foghorn: the manual foghorns are superior to the canister style, because you don't have to worry about the amount of charge left.

EPIRB: an expensive piece of equipment that's invaluable in off-shore situations; check daily and protect against accidental triggering.

person waving arms

Mayday by radio

VHF radio in waterproof bag with spare VHF battery pack.

your arms over your head, and a Mayday call over a radio. All of the above signals are useful during daylight hours and some, like flares, can also be used at night. Other devices you can use for signaling but are not necessarily recognized as distress signals worldwide are strobe lights, mirrors, orange flags or ribbons, and whistles. It's prudent to carry a variety of these devices. Consider keeping them packed in a dry bag or box that you take with you every time you go paddling.

LIGHTNING

Lightning is a powerful and dangerous element for anyone traveling on water. It can begin with little warning and catch you out on the water; you should always consider this situation a true emergency. At the first signs of lightning, you must scurry for cover. You'll need to make every effort possible to get off the water and pull your boat up and secure it.

Lightning occurs when there is a buildup of electrical charges within the towering cumulus cloud. This may discharge within the cloud or between the cloud and the ground (the earth is normally negatively charged). Thunder is the sound we hear when heat energy from a lightning strike is released, creating sound waves. Time the interval between seeing a lightning flash or strike and hearing the thunder associated with it in seconds; then multiply by 0.2 to find out how far, in miles, the thunderhead is from your location.

Head for a low area with bushes and a few trees that are not the tallest in the area. Avoid wide-open spaces such as meadows or bluffs along headlands. Use your life vest as a ground pad and spread out the members in your group, since lightning can splash from its original strike. Stay in a low crouch and keep your feet close together. Try to avoid placing your hands on the ground or on any trees since you do not want to present a path for a strike to travel across your body. Keep metal objects (paddle shaft, flashlight, knife, etc.) away from your position.

CAPSIZE!

If you're smart, your first capsize will be something you've planned and will take place under controlled conditions that allow you to practice a proper wet exit. Good wet exit technique includes leaning forward to free your hips from the seat and clearing the sprayskirt from the coaming before pushing out of the boat.

Learning to get back into your boat by yourself is invaluable. You will be more confident if you know these techniques and are not dependent on others to help you reenter. A solo reentry is a balancing act, and haste is your biggest enemy. You will need to flip your boat over and use your paddle, with an inflated paddle float on one blade, as a supportive outrigger to reenter the cockpit. It is critical that you keep the paddle perpendicular to the boat and the float as far away as possible for the best support. It is usually easiest to do this by clamping the paddle in place behind the rear cockpit coaming or placing the bare paddle blade under the rear deck rigging (photo 1).

1 Position the paddle float perpendicular and fully extended for maximum support as you swim up onto the boat.

2 You may try hooking an ankle on the paddle shaft for additional support.

You'll need to swim up onto the cockpit of the boat and inch on your belly toward the stern until you can fit your feet and then your legs into the cockpit (photo 2). Make sure to put most of your weight on the supported side of the boat. Slide your hand down the paddle shaft and keep an eye on the paddle float at all times—it should never lift from the water, which indicates that your weight has shifted away from its support.

Once you've tucked your feet and legs into the cockpit, you are ready to turn and seat yourself. Turn toward the paddle float, making sure to keep your weight toward that side of the boat (photo 4). Once you're seated, bring the paddle over

Stay low and keep your eyes on the paddle float as you move to the stern on your belly.

3

Turn toward the paddle float and favor that side as you turn in the cockpit.

4

Continue to lean on your paddle shaft and supportive paddle float as you get seated and rearranged in your cockpit.

5

Move your paddle in front of you and lean on it for support as you pump the boat out.

6

your head, place it across the coaming, and use it for support while you pump the boat dry (photos 5–6). If the boat is taking on any water from breaking waves, attach your sprayskirt, leaving just enough room so you can use the bilge pump.

If you need to add a layer of clothes or find a quick snack, it is best to do this while you are being stabilized by the paddle float. Whatever conditions caused your capsize are probably still present.

CAPSIZED PARTNER

The unexpected capsize of someone in your paddling group is a time for action and calm authority. You have to accomplish two things: get the capsized person (we'll call her the "swimmer") back into the boat and empty the water from the boat. The conditions will determine in what order you do these things.

Medical protocol takes precedence over all else. When you first approach the swimmer, first make sure she is OK. (You also do not want to be overturned by a panicked swimmer.) Make sure the swimmer holds onto her boat at all times and keeps a grip on her paddle until you can take it from her. You will need to get to the overturned boat as quickly as possible, so don't waste time trying to paddle to the bow. Grab the overturned boat anywhere and then use your hands to "walk" around the boat to reach the bow.

Position your boat perpendicular to the swimmer's boat and have her hold onto her stern. If you plan to lift the capsized boat, it is helpful to have the swimmer push down as you simultaneously lift the bow and pull it across your cockpit (photo 1). You can then lift the bow until the swimmer's cockpit is clear of the water and roll the boat upright. This will empty the water

If the boat is not heavily loaded, you can lift it to drain water before proceeding with the reentry.

Lean across the swimmer's boat and stabilize it by holding the thighbraces (or inside the forward cockpit coaming) with both hands.

from the boat and make it much easier to proceed. (However, it may not be possible if the boat is heavily loaded. In that case you will have to come alongside the boat, turn it over, and then remove the water after the swimmer has reentered.)

Slide the swimmer's upright boat off your cockpit and bring it alongside and pointing in the opposite direction from your boat (this makes it easier to monitor the swimmer's reentry and protects your fingers). Store the swimmer's paddle with yours under your foredeck rigging. Hold the swimmer's boat with both your hands by grasping the thighbraces or underside of the forward coaming (photo 2). By holding the swimmer's boat firmly and leaning into it, you will provide a stable platform for the swimmer to reenter.

Once the swimmer has reentered (photos 3 and 4), make sure she is seated and ready to paddle. Unless you must leave the area quickly, this is a good time for both you and the swimmer to add another layer of clothes or take a quick snack and water break. Do not let the swimmer begin paddling on her own unless you are sure she is capable of doing so. Another capsize at this point could be disastrous. If needed, you can stabilize her and set up a tow that is appropriate for the conditions (see pages 92–95).

The swimmer should slide her legs into the cockpit and turn toward the rescuer as she reenters her cockpit.

Continue to stabilize the swimmer's boat until she is ready to resume paddling.

RESCUE SLING

A rescue sling is a piece of floating line or webbing that has been formed into a loop about six feet long. This sling is handy for helping a paddler reenter a boat after a capsize or following a swim. The sling is particularly useful during a solo paddle float reentry, since it gives you a boost up onto the boat while it helps lock your paddle into a position perpendicular to the boat. In this case, you can loop the sling over the bare paddle blade (the other blade has a paddle float on it), bring it under the boat, and then loop it over the paddle shaft to create a foot stirrup.

You can also drape a rescue sling around the cockpit coaming and allow it to trail in the water in front of the person reentering the boat. This can be used as an intermediate step when getting back into the boat from the water. If the sling is too long for this, take a few hitches in it to shorten it to a usable length.

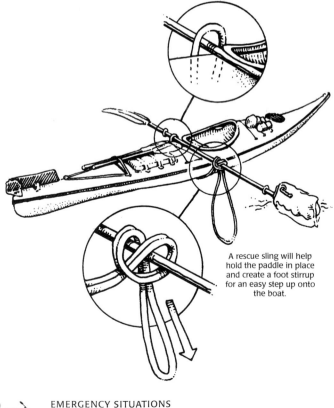

A rescue sling will help hold the paddle in place and create a foot stirrup for an easy step up onto the boat.

LOST KAYAKER

Before setting out, your paddling group should have agreed on group signals (see pages 48–49) and what you will do if someone becomes separated from the group. Doing this in advance will make it easier to act efficiently if someone does get separated from the group. Groups should employ a "buddy" system for keeping track of everyone, especially in low visibility.

Anyone separated from the group should immediately look for a landing spot or find something to use to slow her drift. If there is no landing spot close by, the lost person should hold position by pointing her bow into the wind. She should then sit still and listen for a signal from the group. If she doesn't hear one, she should use the agreed-upon whistle signal and wait for a response. She should continue to signal at regular intervals and wait for the group to find her. If she begins moving it will make the search more difficult.

Group members should determine the time and location the paddler was last seen and then decide on a search method. Individual experience levels will determine how you proceed. It might be better to land some members nearby and appoint a limited number of searchers, especially if the visibility is poor (you don't want more lost people!). Then consider the tidal current and wind direction and begin to narrow the search area. Grid searches are difficult to enact on the water unless conditions are perfect. Instead, consider paddling nearby shorelines in the search area first and signaling at regular intervals. Keep close track of time and mark the areas you have searched.

Consider placing a call on your VHF radio so other boaters can keep an eye out for the lost person. Any radio transmissions should note the color of the boat, clothing, and other factors that might help in the search, as well as the paddler's last known location.

If the conditions deteriorate or you have particular concerns about the lost person (cold temperatures, medical problem, etc.), you should place a call on channel 16 of your VHF radio using the Pan-Pan prefix. Obviously, the exact conditions will dictate the level of urgency you feel is necessary ("Mayday" may even be appropriate). Be as specific as you can about your location and the area that you've searched. You will be told what measures local authorities are taking and what you and other group members can do to help.

WHEN IT'S TIME TO TOW

TOWING IN SEAS

When you must tow another kayak in any seas, the boats must be 20 to 30 feet apart. Following seas can be especially challenging, because the kayak being towed will have a tendency to surf into the towing boat. As the one doing the towing, you might also experience severe jerks on the line as the towed boat is slowed in a trough just as you begin to pick up speed down a wave face. Having a piece of bungee cord built into your towline will help smooth this out.

As the one towing, you will want to make sure you have a way to quickly release the towline from your boat or your waist. You can't take the chance of becoming entangled in the towline, especially if you were to capsize. You can wear the towline around your waist or attach it immediately behind your cockpit, as long as you can reach it easily. Never loop a towline around your shoulder or paddle shaft. You need the forces of the towline centered on the boat or your body, and the line will have to clear the rudder system and any gear on the stern deck. Attach the towline to the towed boat at the bow (photos 1 and 2).

Make sure the paddler being towed is able to remain upright. You should also let him know whether you prefer for him to slowly paddle forward during the tow or store his paddle under the deck rigging (photo 3). It is best to communicate these things *before* you begin the tow.

If additional people towing can help, the job will be less tiring. In a serial tow, two or more tow-boats are hooked in line to the towed boat. You might also choose to use a "husky" tow, which places two people towing at angles off the bow of the boat being towed, forming a V-shaped pull.

You can also use towing to connect paddlers during long crossings or to stabilize a group's speed. Sometimes a tow gives a paddler just enough of a break, and he can continue to paddle throughout the tow.

Clip the towline into a sturdy piece of hardware or line at the bow.

1

Make sure the towline feeds freely (here from a towline worn at the waist).

2

Make sure the boats are separated in any seas to avoid collision. You may also choose to add another tower to the pull for additional help.

3

CLOSE-CONTACT TOWING

If you need to stabilize a towed paddler for a short sprint to land, a close-contact tow is the best choice. This tow uses a much shorter line and the two boats are actually in contact during the tow. You might use a "pigtail" towline off your life vest (photo 1) or attach a painter (length of line) from the towed kayak's bow toggle to a deck attachment on the tow boat.

A close-contact tow allows you to be within reach of the towed paddler, which is invaluable in the case of a medical problem or seasickness, especially if there is not a third paddler available for help. The towed paddler may even lean across the stern deck of the tow boat if needed (photo 2). A close-contact tow is probably not going to be possible in extremely rough conditions and heavy following seas.

Clip the towline into the rigging or other hardware on the forward deck alongside the tower.

1

The short line used in a contact tow allows the towed paddler to be stabilized on the back deck and more easily monitored. The efficiency and practicality of this tow are reduced in strong winds or seas.

2

STABILIZING THE TOWED PADDLER

The best way to stabilize a towed paddler is to get help from another person in the group. This assistant can position her boat alongside the towed boat and attach a short line with a quick release that connects the two. If the assistant must help with the tow, she should position her boat forward of the victim's boat similar to a close-contact tow. If the towed paddler needs monitoring and medical assistance during the tow, the assistant might bring her kayak alongside and just aft of the towed kayak's cockpit. In this way, she can keep a close eye on the towed paddler and make any adjustments as needed.

If there are no other paddlers available for assistance and a close-contact tow is not possible, you can use a paddle with inflated paddle floats on both blades for stability. These serve as buoyant outriggers that will help stabilize the towed kayak. If the towed paddler is not able to hold the paddle in place, attach it through the deck rigging behind or in front of the cockpit. Make sure the paddle shaft will not interfere with the towed paddler's exiting the cockpit in the event of a capsize.

If another paddler is not available for help, you can use inflated paddle floats on both blades of a paddle for stabilization during the tow. If the towed paddler is unable to hold the paddle shaft in place, it can be secured under the deck rigging.

Going Ashore

GETTING THERE

LANDING SITES

Your choice of landing sites will depend on whether you are planning to stay overnight, stopping for a lunch break, or need access to emergency assistance. Any landing site must be accessible by kayak under reasonable conditions. While gently sloping beaches are not always available, you should look for locations that are accessible at most, if not all, stages of the tidal range. You don't want to be stuck waiting for a rising tide to release you from your landing site.

By reviewing chart and tide tables, you'll be able to tell what sites might be appropriate. Along with paying attention to tidal height, look for gentle slopes and minimal exposure to the wind. You don't want to land or launch from a lee shore (exposed to the wind) in heavy weather, especially if the fetch is sizable. If you're spending the night, keep the weather report in mind when you choose your landing site, since the next morning's weather will also affect the site's suitability. Obviously, you must have permission to land unless it is public property or you are going ashore for emergency purposes. Before setting out, note on your chart all areas where you have the right to land. Draw boundaries for public lands and any private properties you have access to by permission of the landowner.

If you are making a landing for emergency purposes, look for access to roads or houses. This will make it easier to contact emergency personnel and get them to your site.

Planning your landing with the tides in mind is a must in many areas. Otherwise you'll be faced with a long and ugly slog to your destination.

Your landing site may be a temporary parking place at low tide. Make sure any rising tide or surge will not float boats away from these sites.

If you're lucky you'll be able to access a soft and gradual slope ideal for landing kayaks.

LANDING IN SURF

You'll need patience and impeccable timing to make a soft, successful landing in surf. If you are traveling in a heavily loaded kayak, you will need to be even more cautious—not only is a loaded kayak slower to respond to corrections, but the momentum of a loaded kayak as it gains speed down a wave face can be frightening and destructive. You do not want to get clipped in the surf by a loaded kayak.

Before you attempt to land, sit outside the surf zone and time the waves to discern a rhythm to their sets. Pick out the areas where the break seems gentler and less confusing. As you begin to pick your way toward the beach, let each wave pass under you and try to ride in on the wave's backface for a soft landing. You want to avoid gaining speed down the face of the wave or burying the bow of your boat (pearling).

Unlike when paddling in following seas, losing forward momentum is not a problem in surf, so don't hesitate to back-paddle to let a wave pass or to stall for a better position. If you get caught sideways to the wave, or broach, lean into the wave and brace on its crest until you can regain a position perpendicular to the wave or actually land.

Once your kayak grounds out you will have to move quickly or you may be swept back into the surf. Get out of the boat, grab the bow toggle, and run directly away from the reach of the water if possible. If the boat is heavily loaded this may be more of a crawl, and a loaded double kayak will require some serious hefting. If the boat is lifted by a wave and flung about, let go—you can be seriously injured trying to control it. It's best to let it be tossed around and then retrieve it.

It works well to let an experienced paddler land first and then direct others into shore and help them get out of their boats. You can use hand or paddle signals to direct each paddler in and time his or her landing.

don't be afraid to back-paddle and let a wave pass to stall for a better position

Pick your way through the surf and try to time your landing to arrive on the back of a wave. Get out quickly and pull boat away from the water.

PUBLIC ACCESS

Your right to walk, fish, hunt, or kayak through a piece of private property has largely been a matter left to individual states and has resulted in several landmark challenges over the years. In general, though, you shouldn't be on private property unless you have the permission of the property owner. It sounds simple, but kayakers are notorious for what we may optimistically call *permissive trespass*—a nice way of saying that we've gotten away with it in the past and think we can continue to do so in the future.

Many remote locations, especially islands, offer refuge to passing kayakers and may rarely be visited by their owners. However, this doesn't give you the right to camp overnight on their shores, even if you got away with it last year. For one thing, ownership changes hands, and access might even be under negotiation.

Many states have water trail organizations that combine both public and privately owned properties that are open to members. Check to see if there is a water trail in your area and consider joining. Often, access to various locations will change each year, so membership must be renewed to gain updated information. It can be a shock to arrive at your landing site to find a new home under construction and the shoreline papered with No Trespassing signs.

Check with local officials to find out what the state law is for access to beaches and other coastal sites. Some are quite permissive, allowing unrestricted access below the highest high tide line; others restrict this access to colonial uses of "fishing, fowling, and navigation" only. The important things are to be informed and to act responsibly; your actions may affect sea kayakers who travel these same waters after you.

Most public lands have access information posted. This might include carrying capacity and overnight stay limits. Use local sources (outfitters, water trail organizations, state agencies, etc.) to get this information in advance of your trip.

CAMPING

CHOOSING A CAMPSITE

While the nature of the particular geographical region will play a major role, several features are universal to good campsites. To choose the safest and most pleasant site, consider the following things.

Your campsite should be protected from heavy weather. Look at the topography. Does it channel wind and cold air down to your campsite or protect you from these elements? If it is a warm-weather site, does it allow fresh breezes that will cool you and keep the bugs away? Don't camp beneath tall trees that might draw lightning strikes or be a danger in high winds.

You might have other requirements for a perfect campsite: a quiet place to sit alone and watch the stars, a view across the water, or the presence of edible plants.

Choose a campsite well away from any wildlife trails (look for tracks, spoor, nests, and scratches or gnawed spots on nearby trees).

A good campsite will utilize established tent areas and blend into the surroundings. Pull boats well above the reach of the water and make sure all gear is secured for the evening. If campfires are allowed and appropriate, is there sufficient deadwood in the area and an established fire ring? Does the site allow you to be close to the boats, and is there a place to pull them well above the high tide line and out of the wind? Will you have privacy from other campers or nearby roads or houses? Check the ground for a level spot suitable for a tent. Avoid gullies and sites that will collect water or that sit alongside small streams or seasonal runs that might flood during a rainstorm. Make sure there are no poisonous plants like poison ivy or oak in the area.

SETTING UP CAMP

When you set up camp, make sure the kayaks are well above the reach of the water and secured from any strong winds. After you've unpacked your gear, make sure all the hatches are sealed and a cockpit cover in place (or use your sprayskirt and cinch the waist) to keep out animals and insects.

If there are clearly established tent sites, use them to avoid compacting new areas of ground. Do not trench a tent site; instead, choose a piece of ground that will allow water to drain from under your tent if needed.

Establish your kitchen and dining area fairly nearby with good wind protection and no overhanging trees. If you need additional wind protection, rig a tarp between two trees as a windbreak. Do not start a fire or use a camp stove under a low-hanging tarp or tent fly. You can capture the fire's heat by positioning a tarp with the open end facing the fire and the other sides enclosed if needed. If the area is sandy, try to get the prep and cooking surfaces off the ground—your meal will be less crunchy.

Keep rain gear, flashlights, and additional clothing at the campsite so you won't have to root around in the boats at night. If needed, decide where you will establish your latrine and make sure everyone is familiar with how to properly dispose of waste. If there is a common path to the latrine area, hang up the toilet paper roll or some other marker that can be taken when someone is using the area and returned when she is finished. It's always nice to have the place to yourself for a while!

Before lights out, make sure you've stored all the food and kitchen gear away from any marauding wildlife (but not in your tent!). Stow any loose pieces of gear and make sure all tarps and tents are battened down for the evening. Make sure your boats are secure.

USING SALT WATER

Salt water may be of no use as drinking water, but you can use it for cleaning, washing, and for certain cooking chores. If freshwater is precious—and it usually is on sea kayaking trips—you can do all the dishwashing and cleaning with salt water. Boil salt water before using it for rinsing. Often a good scrub with coarse sand and a rinse in boiled salt water is sufficient

Freshwater can be conserved by using salt water and a sand and gravel scrub for meal cleanup. Make sure there are no water quality problems in the area, and consider a freshwater or boiled saltwater rinse for the final cleaning stage.

for most kitchen cleanup. If you prefer, you can follow this method with a quick freshwater rinse.

You can use salt water for cooking anything that doesn't absorb the bulk of the water but must be simmered or boiled. Salt water works great for corn on the cob, shellfish, and fresh beans and peas. Do not use it for rice or in recipes with flour or meal. If there are any concerns about the water quality in the area where you're paddling, don't chance using salt water at all for cooking or cleaning. It is better to be conservative than to cut a trip short because of illness.

If you use salt water for washing dishes or yourself you might appreciate a bit of soap. Choose a biodegradable version to avoid dumping any more pollutants into the water—though even biodegradable soaps require time to break down. Dr. Bronner's liquid soap works great, and you can use it to wash your hair and even brush your teeth!

HOW MUCH WATER?

Unless you are sure you can replenish your potable water supply along the way, you will need to carry the entire trip's water from the start. This will probably constitute the heaviest gear in your kayak, but you can't scrimp on water. Plan on a minimum of 1 gallon per person per day. In hot, dry environments this may go as high as 1.5 gallons per person per day. For a multiday trip this will look like an enormous amount of water. Unless you have a lot of other sodas or juices packed for meals and snacks, you'll need to plan on these amounts.

Everyone on the trip will need at least one water bottle that can be refilled several times a day. Soft-sided water carriers will

Water will constitute the heaviest and bulkiest category during packing. This photo shows the water planned for two paddlers for a two-day trip (6 gallons—about 50 pounds' worth). Unless you are sure you can re-provision along the way, never skimp on the water.

make packing easier, but you will need to take great care not to puncture or abrade any seams. Pack one water carrier in an accessible location for refilling other water bottles throughout the day. In hot climates, keep a water bottle in a day hatch or nestled in the cockpit along the centerline to keep the water cooler.

LEAVE-NO-TRACE KAYAKING

Sea kayaks leave no oil sheen or noise in their wake. Sea kayakers should be as low impact as their crafts, leaving no trace of their passing by adhering to low-impact techniques, which take into account the land, water, and wildlife before every action and minimize the impact of humans whenever possible.

It is always exciting to pull into a landing site, soaking up the surroundings and eyeing the views as you set up camp. Even though you know that others have camped here before you, you don't want to be reminded of it by signs that they have carelessly left behind. When you set up camp, try to minimize your impact on the vegetation and on any others who might be passing by your location. Visual pollution may not harm the land, but it jars the senses of others enjoying the outdoors.

When you break camp, remove all trash, even if it was left by others. If you've created a temporary fire ring below the high tide line, dismantle it and spread the remains around for the next tide to scour clean. Try to leave your site as pristine and untouched as you would like to find it on your arrival.

GRAY-WATER DISPOSAL

The proper disposal of dishwater and other liquids that do not include human wastes or trash varies by location. In areas with sufficient soil depth and organic material, you may pour gray water along a shallow trough and bury it, as long as it's at least a hundred yards from any freshwater source. In some backwoods sites, it's recommended that gray water be poured into the established fire ring.

Soap is usually the strongest contaminant in any gray-water disposal. If you do not use soap, the disposal of gray water is simplified: you can pour it out well away from shore into an active water column (where there is plenty of both horizontal and vertical water movement). Never dispose of gray water in a body of water where there is little or no water movement. Avoid areas where there are shellfish or other intertidal creatures. Often, deep sand is a good surface for absorbing gray water. If there are any food scraps from dish rinsing, this should be taken into consideration if wildlife is nearby. You might need to filter the water and pack out the food scraps.

Gray water may be paddled away from shore and disposed of in an active water column. If this is not possible, pour through sand below the high tide line or into an established fire ring. Never pour gray water into a tidal pool.

WASTE DISPOSAL

Here's a topic for your after-dinner conversation—what to do with human wastes during a kayak trip! Liquid human wastes may be disposed of over the side of the boat into an active water column while under way, but what about solid wastes? You need to find out the appropriate method of storage and disposal for the area where you are paddling.

In rich soil layers, you might be able to dig cat holes, shallow holes where you deposit your waste and cover it with soil. If the nutrient levels in the soil are high, this waste will rapidly break down into organic matter within days. Burn or carry out toilet paper.

However, many islands, especially those along the upper East Coast, have only thin, nutrient-starved soils that cannot break down human wastes quickly. Burying waste is not an option at these sites. Instead, you will need to carry your wastes out and dispose of them in appropriate ways on land (at marine pump-out stations or your own toilet, not in a landfill).

There are several ingenious methods for dealing with this problem. Some kayakers use tight-sealing plastic containers lined with cat litter or peat moss. Others use paper bags for individual deposits and store them in a plastic-lined ammo can throughout the trip. There are also commercial products available, like the Boom Box (shown below), a portable toilet that is small enough to fit in some stern hatches or ride on the stern deck. Pack rubber gloves and antiseptic wipes for handling the containers—it isn't that difficult to make these systems work once you accept that you need to carry out all your wastes.

If you've ever visited a campsite to find toilet paper blowing around and little mounds of waste in the woods, you'll appreciate removing this problem from those places we love to explore. Check with local water trail organizations, paddlesports shops, and outfitters to find out what is appropriate for your planned trip. If in doubt, pack it out.

WILLDLIFE

SEA BIRDS

The incredible variety of sea birds that frequent coastal waters makes for great birdwatching. Bird behaviors range from the solitary shyness of a juvenile loon to the great rafts of eider that form just offshore during breeding season. All of these birds deserve to be given a wide berth and their nesting and breeding sites left undisturbed.

Spring and early summer bring a frenzy of nest building as many sea birds prepare for young that have mortality rates as high as 70 percent. Mothers may sit on the nests without break or share this duty with their mate. To disturb this nesting behavior can result in a deserted nest and no young for that year. Often, watchful gulls will feed on an unprotected nest where the parent was flushed by a careless human. If you see birds on the nest or suspect that they are close by, avoid the area entirely. Your presence will only endanger the young.

When young sea birds begin swimming, their mothers corral and protected them as they learn to feed from the sea. Typically the young are too buoyant to dive if attacked. This is a

In many locations, the peak paddling season coincides with critical bird nesting and rearing periods. You must be careful to avoid nesting sites or separating young from their mothers on the water.

Great Blue Heron

dangerous time, since it is easy for young to become separated from the mother, and they rarely last long if they do. For instance, it is common for gulls to stalk rafts of eider and scoop the young from the water at the slightest opportunity. Kayakers often play an unwitting hand in creating this opportune moment when they paddle too close and accidentally separate the young from their mother.

Many islands and shoreline sites are closed to the public for most of the summer to protect rookeries and fragile nesting sites of herons, osprey, eagles, and colonial nesting sea birds. Some birds, like great blue herons, have young on the nest as late as mid-August. Please abide by any posting or restrictive visitation guidelines when you plan to explore coastal areas.

BIRD NESTING AREA

PLEASE:
DO NOT PROCEED BEYOND THIS SIGN.

We need your help to avoid disturbance to nesting birds occupying this area.

THANK YOU

MARINE MAMMALS

As kayakers, we yearn to observe marine mammals and can be delighted for hours watching them play or feed. A kayak offers an intimate view of wildlife and may allow close approaches to these creatures. But too often, these close approaches disrupt natural behaviors and we end up observing flight and stress instead.

The best way to observe marine mammals is through a good pair of binoculars. You'll be able to watch them behave naturally and learn more about them than you would if you sneaked up close for a momentary glance before flushing them from the area. Any careless actions on your part may well be illegal. The Marine Mammal Protection Act, passed in 1972, recommends that people maintain a distance of 100 yards and prohibits "harassment," defined as any act causing animals to alter their natural behavior.

As with sea birds, you want to be particularly careful to avoid separating mothers from their young, which stresses the offspring and may affect their survival. Young whales, otters, sea lions, and seals are all dependent on their mothers for survival, and this bond must not be disturbed. Give haulout ledges a wide berth to avoid flushing seals and sea lions. These breaks from the water are important to the animals, and if young are present, they could be trampled if you flush the adults.

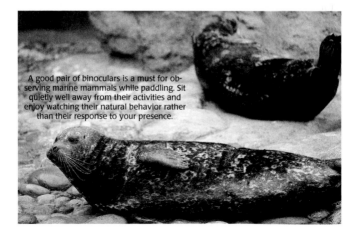

A good pair of binoculars is a must for observing marine mammals while paddling. Sit quietly well away from their activities and enjoy watching their natural behavior rather than their response to your presence.

STRANDED ANIMALS

At some point you may come across what appears to be a stranded animal—a seal pup left alone on a ledge or an osprey chick that flounders along the shoreline. Do not approach the animals in these situations. Instead, move quietly from the area and try to observe the scene through your binoculars. Often, the mother may be close by but afraid to approach because of your presence.

If you are convinced that you are observing a stranded animal, make a note of the exact location and contact local authorities. Most states have contacts for just this situation, such as a university program, a conservation organization, or an aquarium. These are the folks that have the training to deal with stranded animals and increase the likelihood of their survival. Do not remove stranded animals yourself: call the proper authorities—the local coast guard station or sheriff's office.

Quietly leave an area if you think you have sighted a young stranded animal. Often, the mother is close by and waiting for you to leave before she returns to her young.

Field Repairs

BOAT REPAIRS

LEAKS

At the lunch break, you discover that there's more than a mere sprinkle of water in one of your hatches. You sponge things out, look around in the compartment, and then replace the hatch cover, making sure it is well seated. At the end of the day, you find more water and think you've got a leak somewhere. But water in a hatch might also come from items stored in the hatch, like a leaky water bottle or soft cooler, or condensation produced by thawing food or differences in the water and air temperatures. Try to rule out these possibilities before proceeding.

You'll need a systematic approach to find a leak. They can occur through bulkhead sealant breaks, a corrupt seam or hole

To find a boat leak, submerge areas and look for the source of the problem. There are a variety of potential culprits, so you'll need to narrow the choices with each step.

in the end pour on a composite boat, pinholes in the plastic of a polyethylene boat, through a rudder attachment at the stern, or through some leak in the hatch cover, gasket, or piece of deck hardware.

If the problem is a bulkhead sealant gap, a leak in the hatch could occur only if there was water in the cockpit at some point. If your cockpit's been dry all day, you can rule out the bulkhead and its sealant. The other possibilities will require you to empty the hatch (leaving the cover off), place the affected end in the water, and push down while watching for any seepage of water into the hatch. Roll the boat on its shoulder so the seam is submerged on each side. If you're lucky, you'll see a wet area on the cloth or a dribble through a pinhole in the plastic, and you've found the culprit.

If you can't find the problem by pushing the hull under water, you'll have to fill the hatch with water and then look for any seepage on the outside. Dry the outside of the boat and then dump a bucket of water in the hatch. Tilt the boat toward one end and hold it. If this doesn't pinpoint the leak, tilt the boat toward the other end. If no leak is apparent, replace the hatch cover and fasten tightly. Now turn the boat over and see if water seeps through any deck hardware or around the hatch gasket.

Sometimes pinhole leaks are nearly impossible to find. You may have to wait until you return home to do a more thorough investigation under better light and more controlled conditions.

Repair Kit Contents (store in wide-mouth Nalgene 1-quart bottle)

✓ duct tape (wrap around bottle)

✓ screws (machine and self-tapping)

✓ screw driver, small tools (4-inch Vise-Grips, stubby screwdrivers)

✓ bolts and locknuts

✓ cable swages

✓ vinyl patch repair kit

✓ tube of Aquaseal

✓ tire patch kit (latex gaskets)

✓ wire ties and shrink tubing

✓ two-part epoxy putty

✓ eyeglass repair kit

✓ extra rudder or skeg cable

✓ lighter for sealing ends of line

✓ extra gear eyes (deck loops)

✓ rudder track screws with O-rings

✓ replacement buckles and ladderlocks for hatch straps

✓ spring button for take-apart paddle

✓ various pieces of small line

✓ graphite powder

✓ fine sandpaper

COMPOSITE (CLOTH AND RESIN) KAYAKS

Scratches and dings in your boat are signs of good kayaking times; they say you've been somewhere and are putting your equipment to good use. But occasionally, you land really hard or glance off a submerged rock and hear the telltale crunch that gelcoat makes when it gives in to the outside force. It's time to take a look at the damage.

Look both inside and out to determine the level of damage to your composite kayak. Cloth and resin layups are surprisingly tough, so you may have just created a deep gouge or scratch that you can fix at your leisure, getting the gelcoat match perfect. If there are spider-web lines around the point of impact and only small chunks of gelcoat missing, you may be OK until you get home but will need to keep a close eye on the area. If you can see daylight, you'll have to fix it in the field.

If you can flex the cloth with your finger but not see a hole, protect this soft spot until it can be properly repaired. Dry the area and use fine sandpaper to rough up the edges around the wound on both the inside and outside surfaces. Then apply duct tape with rounded edges over the wound on both sides (you may have to replace the outside layer each day). Make sure any gear that comes into contact with the damaged area will not push against the soft spot. After you resume paddling, check to make sure there isn't anything more than light seepage from the wound.

If you do see a hole, you can try using several layers of crossed duct tape, but you'll need to check it regularly and make sure you aren't taking on water. You might also take the time to glue a vinyl patch (like you'd use on a dry bag or inflatable mattress) over the area that you can later remove for a full repair. Many kayakers carry a two-part epoxy putty that can even set up on wet surfaces. This works fairly well, but you'll need to grind away the putty before you can repair the outside area to match the existing gelcoat.

You can make a temporary field repair to gelcoat damage by crossing duct tape over the wound. Round the edges of the tape before applying.

This will need to be monitored and may have to be replaced daily.

PLASTIC KAYAKS

Polyethylene boats are remarkably durable, so it is unlikely that you will face any major repairs. You might find a pinhole leak or, more likely, have to fix a leak around a piece of deck hardware where the hole has enlarged over time. You can repair plastic with other plastic scraps and a heat source, but this is not a typical field repair. You'll just want to stabilize things until you can make a full repair at home.

Often, a glob of Shoe Goo or marine sealant will save the day on small pinholes or cracks. If you're faced with an enlarged hole around a piece of deck hardware, try seating the screw in a thin rubber washer to seal the hole. You can then cover it with sealant for added protection. In a pinch, you can even run a screw with a rubber washer into a pinhole to seal it.

Duct tape repairs are always possible but may not stick well to the surface of the plastic. If you lightly sand the area and clean it with an alcohol swab, you'll increase the likelihood that the tape will stick and stay. Make sure to round the edges of the duct tape and keep a close eye on things, since it may need replacing before the trip is done.

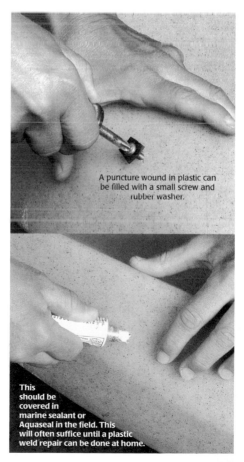

A puncture wound in plastic can be filled with a small screw and rubber washer.

This should be covered in marine sealant or Aquaseal in the field. This will often suffice until a plastic weld repair can be done at home.

RUDDER AND SKEG JAMS

As soon as you add moving parts to a kayak, you must face the inevitable—they will jam, break, or throw themselves overboard in order to maximize your frustration. Rudders and skegs are prone to jamming, so you'll probably get used to making these minor repairs over years of paddling. You should always carry extra screws, locknuts, washers, cable swages, and even an extra rudder cable in your repair kit along with a small pair of Vise-Grips and a screwdriver.

Often, rudders or skegs jam because they are full of sand or have a small pebble wedged in their workings. Dip the stern under water and try to remove any sand from the area. Squirt a water bottle at the area to force water into the workings for a deeper cleaning job. You might also work a knife blade along the rudder cams or skeg blade to dislodge any small pebbles. Try to manually move the blade of the rudder or skeg and see if there is still any obstruction or if it moves freely after this cleaning.

If the blade is still jammed, you'll need to dismantle the rudder or skeg mechanism for a full repair. Before you do this,

Often a thorough washing around the rudder or skeg blade will correct a jam. Other culprits include small pebbles that can be removed with a knife, and kinks in the rudder or skeg line.

make sure you have the knowledge and tools (not to mention patience and time) to get the repair done under the circumstances. It might be better to declare the rudder or skeg inoperable and wait until you get home to do the repair under more comfortable conditions. Of course, the damage might be such that you must make some adjustment before you can continue paddling.

Before you dismantle things, place a tarp or ground cloth beneath the boat to catch any loose parts. You don't want to be picking through sand and dry seaweed to find the last missing screw. If you must dismantle the rudder cams or any downhaul/uphaul lines, make sure you have drawn their correct orientation before you do so.

Common problems (besides grit and small pebbles) that you should check on faulty rudders and skegs:

- rudder line that has jumped the track on a cam
- kinks in the skeg line
- downhaul or uphaul lines that have frayed, broken, or are misaligned
- a machine screw on the cam has fallen out or stripped
- the clevis pin or ring has fallen off the rudder pin
- the rudder base or attachment has cracked and loosened
- the skeg blade is loose or unattached from its cable
- a rudder cable screw has been lost
- a rudder cable swage or the cable itself has broken

A loop of line tied through a small hole in the skeg will help release the skeg when it's jammed with small pebbles.

To make it easy to find the string, mark the position of the skeg with a small patch of colored tape.

Near the bottom corner of the skeg drill a $\frac{3}{16}$-inch hole. Tie a loop of braided fishing line or other durable cord through the hole so it hangs down about 2 inches.

JAMMED FOOT BRACES

Sand and grit are usually the culprits when it comes to a jammed foot brace. Check to see if it is the pedal or the sliding track (on rudder systems only) that is jammed. You can often hear it crunch as you try to slide the foot brace along its track or alter the placement of a foot pedal. Try dunking the cockpit and vigorously sloshing water around to wash the grit from the area. If this doesn't work, use your water bottle to aim a stream of water over the area and flush out the grit.

If your foot brace track or pedal is still jammed, check a couple of other possibilities. The pedal might not be properly seated in the track. Some pedals are fitted into a deeply grooved track and will need to be shoehorned back into the track. Other styles click along a notched track and are held in place by screws. These screws can loosen and cause the pedal to jam when pressure is applied.

On a ruddered boat, sometimes the pedal can be adjusted but the track won't slide. Check to make sure that any screws that attach the tracks to the boat aren't interfering with the movement of the tracks. An outside anchoring screw might be just a little bit too long or the track screw that attaches the track to its plate has backed out of its hole. If it's the anchoring screw, add a small rubber washer for spacing to solve the problem; if it's the track screw, simply tighten it.

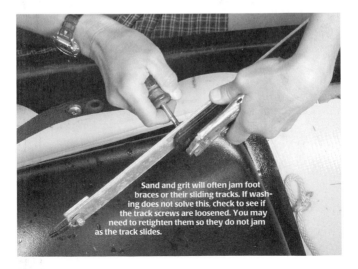

Sand and grit will often jam foot braces or their sliding tracks. If washing does not solve this, check to see if the track screws are loosened. You may need to retighten them so they do not jam as the track slides.

BULKHEAD REPAIRS

You should regularly check the sealant used around bulkheads for cracks and separations. The differential heating and cooling of the hull and the sealant will often require you to reseal your bulkheads at least once a year (plastic boats are especially prone to this). If the sealant has become brittle, it is best to remove it and completely reseal the bulkhead, but do this at home where you can keep things clean, dry, and warm. Your field repair kit is probably stocked with only a small tube of sealant for minor repairs, anyway.

Before you fix any bad spots in the bulkhead sealant, make sure the area is clean and dry. Daub marine sealant into suspicious areas and smooth it with your finger. Make sure the bulkhead is not misaligned or canted from its correct position, which could open up a gap. If it is, you'll need to gently tap it into place and then repair any openings in the sealant. If you have a fiberglass bulkhead, you'll need to use resin to repair any leaks, though a piece of duct tape works nicely in the field.

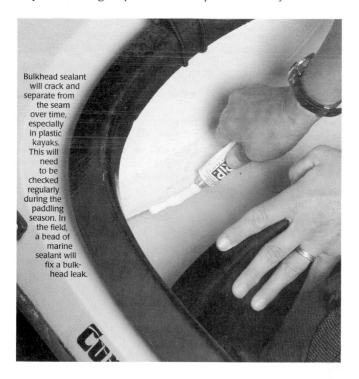

Bulkhead sealant will crack and separate from the seam over time, especially in plastic kayaks. This will need to be checked regularly during the paddling season. In the field, a bead of marine sealant will fix a bulkhead leak.

ACCESSORY REPAIRS

PADDLE BREAKS

You can repair a paddle break much as you would a broken bone. After removing any splinters, fit the ends back together and then stabilize the break. You can use a couple of tongue depressors, Popsicle sticks, or even plastic knives as splints and then wrap the break tightly with duct tape (around the shaft and in lengthwise strips).

If the break is at the paddle throat, it may not be possible to splint it. You can try to glue the blade spline into the shaft and then wrap the throat with duct tape, but the pressures of paddling will probably rebreak it. This is why carrying a spare paddle is sound advice. Any chips or fractures in a composite blade should be treated as a cloth and resin repair.

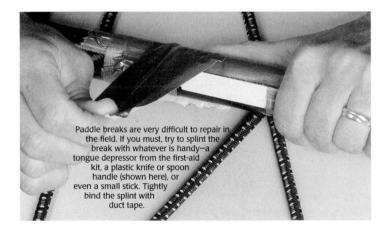

Paddle breaks are very difficult to repair in the field. If you must, try to splint the break with whatever is handy—a tongue depressor from the first-aid kit, a plastic knife or spoon handle (shown here), or even a small stick. Tightly bind the splint with duct tape.

JAMMED PADDLE FERRULES

If the paddle is jammed together in the correct orientation for your use, don't mess with it until the trip is over. After all, a one-piece paddle is hardly a problem when you're paddling, but one that you damaged while trying to twist it apart could be. If the paddle is frozen at some partial position, hold the paddle underwater or make sure it is cooled and then wet it down with freshwater for lubrication. Try to separate it by anchoring one blade between your feet and twisting the other, or use a person on either end while someone holds in the spring button.

If the spring button has jammed inside the shaft, retrieve it with your finger or a stick. Clean it and then work it back and forth through the shaft hole until it pops in and out smoothly. If it keeps jamming, use some fine sandpaper on the hole, but be very careful—you don't want to enlarge it and create a loose joint.

Never use a lubricant like WD-40 on jammed ferrules or joints—it will attract and hold grit and other debris in place and eventually abrade the ferrule. Instead, use graphite powder to dust the joint and ferrule to prevent a future jam. A thorough cleaning with freshwater will do wonders for your paddle and keep it from getting the sticky saltwater deposits that cause many jams.

Jammed ferrules are usually caused by sticky saltwater residue and grit in the joint. Thoroughly clean the joint and check the spring button. It may need to be reseated in the hole.

VINYL (DRY BAGS, ETC.)

Dry bags, soft coolers, and inflatable mattresses often get tears or abrasions that can be fixed with a vinyl patch. You can buy these patch kits at camping or paddlesports shops, or you can simply carry extra vinyl, vinyl adhesive, and alcohol swabs in your repair kit. For field repairs, it is best to get quick-drying vinyl adhesives that do not require heat for curing.

A small hole or tear in a dry bag or inflatable mattress can be repaired with vinyl adhesive and a small vinyl patch. Vinyl patch kits are readily available in most outdoor gear stores and can be stashed in your repair kit. If you do not have one, you may patch the tear with a dab of Shoe Goo or Aquaseal and cover with duct tape for an easy field repair.

Clean the area with an alcohol swab and let it air dry. Work some adhesive into the edges of the tear; then coat the patch with the adhesive and place it over the repair area. Let this dry overnight and try to take it easy on this piece of equipment for a day or so.

DRY SUITS AND DRY TOPS

It's unlikely that you'll be able or even prepared to do a gasket replacement in the field. Instead, you'll need to cover any holes and try to stabilize any tears so they don't pull farther apart. Taking good care of latex gaskets will increase their lifespan significantly. Keep them protected from the sun whenever possible and coat them with 303 Aerospace Protectant, a UV-inhibiting compound. Before you don or remove a dry top or dry suit, remove jewelry, watches, or anything that might snag on a gasket. Hold the gasket open and then slip it on rather than yanking it down by the outer material. If you're nursing an injured gasket through the remainder of a trip, you'll need to be particularly careful. Use talc on yourself and the gasket to ease it across your skin and prevent tearing.

If you have a small hole in a gasket, daub it with some Aquaseal (a viscous sealant available at most camping and paddlesports shops) and then let it dry before covering with duct tape (round the edges). This should hold until you finish your trip. If there is a tear where the latex meets the material of the dry suit, you'll need to use several layers of tape both inside and out to keep the separation from spreading. If there's a tear in the latex alone, close it with Aquaseal and then protect it with duct tape on both sides. If you can get your hands on a bicycle tire patch kit, this will work better and be more comfortable against your skin than the sealant-and-duct-tape repair.

Gasket repairs may be tricky in the field. If the tear is small, you can use a bike tire patch kit for a quick fix. You'll need to treat the gasket gingerly until you can replace it at home.

A piece of advice: Keep sunscreen, cosmetics, and insect repellents away from your dry suit. These compounds will disintegrate latex gaskets and leave you with a black, gooey mess. There is no field repair for this!

NEOPRENE

Modern wet suits are made of a closed-cell material with a nylon skin, and it is the nylon skin that is exposed to the most wear and tear. You can do most repairs with a bead of Aquaseal.

If the tear has gone entirely through the wet suit material, sew it back together by hand and then finish it with Aquaseal. If the tear was particularly nasty or there's a hole, you may want to cover the repair with a temporary duct tape patch until you return home. Stabilize the tear with a few stopper stitches at each end; then apply Aquaseal and let it cure before covering with duct tape.

When you return home, remove the duct tape and clean the area before using an iron-on patch (available at any scuba shop) for a complete repair. The longer you leave the duct tape in place, the more difficult it will be to prep the area for a complete repair.

Tears and punctures can often be repaired with Aquaseal and duct tape. If the damage is greater, you may need to stitch the tear before sealing and applying duct tape to protect the area.

First Aid

MUSCLES AND JOINTS

WRIST ACHES

Most wrist aches are caused by poor technique and a death grip on the paddle. To avoid wrist aches or keep from inflaming an existing one, learn to relax your grip on the paddle and even open your upper hand during your forward stroke. Make sure that the back of your hand is in line with your forearm and there is no torque from side to side as you paddle throughout the day.

Another cause of wrist aches is the use of lightweight but less flexible materials, like graphite, in the manufacture of paddles. You can't beat the feather weight of graphite, but it is brittle, which means more of the stroke snap is absorbed by your wrists, elbows, and shoulders. Newer graphite shafts with more flex are being developed, but you may still have to deal with joint aches on long trips. You can lessen the impact of this by wimping out at the catch of your stroke. As you plant the paddle

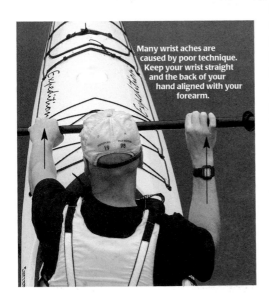

Many wrist aches are caused by poor technique. Keep your wrist straight and the back of your hand aligned with your forearm.

blade during your forward stroke, let your torso slouch just as the paddle catches the water; then follow through with your normal torso rotation. This is not good paddling technique, but it is a way to lessen the jolt on your joints from a stiff paddle.

Once you're off the water, ice or cool your wrists and minimize any side-to-side motion you'll need to put them through (let someone else hammer in the tent stakes or stir the stew). Stretch your wrists before you resume paddling and repeat several times over the course of the day by doing this exercise: hook your pinkie over the edge of the coaming, stretch your fingers and thumbs out, and hold for ten seconds; then relax.

SHOULDER ACHES

If you think a stiff paddle shaft may be at the root of your shoulder ache, then use the same wimpy catch during your forward stroke that helps protect an aching wrist. Poor torso rotation can also cause shoulder aches. If you let the paddle trail behind you with each stroke but never follow with your torso, you will stress the shoulder joint. Do this thousands of times over the course of a day, and you're bound to be hurting. In general, keep your shoulders square with the paddle shaft and your elbows low and close to your side, especially during any braces in surf.

Try to relax your shoulders over the course of the day by rolling them forward and then backwards like an exaggerated shrug. Avoid high-angle or sprint strokes and make sure to watch your paddle blade in the water, which helps protect your shoulders by aligning your torso with the paddle shaft.

DO NOT allow your shoulder to be placed in this sort of unprotected position. Keep the paddle shaft out in front of your torso and rotate your torso to move the paddle shaft.

DISLOCATED SHOULDER

A dislocated shoulder is a serious injury and one that is often tended in the field by kayakers. A dislocation occurs when the ball of the shoulder joint slips from its usual spot nested in the socket. This stresses the connective tissue and can trigger a lot of pain until the joint is realigned. The cessation of pain is apparent if you've ever seen someone have her shoulder popped back in place.

Most shoulder dislocations cause the head of the humerus (upper arm bone) to snap forward and out of socket (an anterior dislocation). You can actually see the uneven protrusion, and the victim will usually cradle her arm to prevent any movement. If you can get the injured paddler to medical help quickly, stabilize the injury by wrapping a compression bandage around the shoulder and torso and creating a supportive sling.

If you are unable to reach medical help within three hours, consider treating the dislocation. Quite frankly, most injured paddlers in this situation will demand that you set things right, since every movement is very painful. Many kayakers have experienced or observed dislocated shoulders, so a group member might be knowledgeable and comfortable with performing the task of setting the shoulder. If you have any doubt about a fracture or other complications, continue to stabilize the joint as if it were a fracture and proceed to find medical assistance.

To reset a dislocated shoulder, wilderness medicine texts recommend that the injured person lie down on a flat surface that lets her arm dangle free. In the field you may have to improvise with a piece of ledge, a large log, or even the stern deck of a boat. Hang some weight that creates a gentle downward pressure from

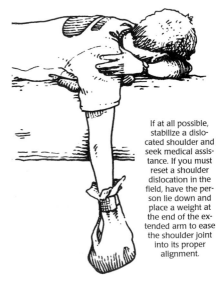

If at all possible, stabilize a dislocated shoulder and seek medical assistance. If you must reset a shoulder dislocation in the field, have the person lie down and place a weight at the end of the extended arm to ease the shoulder joint into its proper alignment.

the dangling hand. This will ease the joint back into correct position with the least trauma. Immediately stabilize the shoulder with a compression wrap and ice or cool the joint until you can get to a medical facility.

SPRAINED ANKLE

Sprained and turned ankles often happen when a kayaker is walking across the slippery slopes of seaweed-covered rocks. A minor turn may require only a pause to gather one's wits and continue on. A sprain will produce immediate swelling and a good deal of pain and must be dealt with quickly.

Elevate the ankle and begin to ice the area. If no ice is available, fill bags with cool water or position water bottles around the ankle. You can also submerge the ankle in cold seawater, though it is difficult to do this and elevate it at the same time. Once the swelling is under control, use a compression bandage and continue to elevate the joint. A severe sprain will most likely incapacitate a paddler and require evacuation.

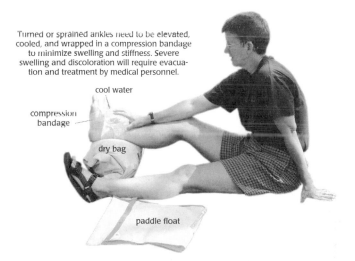

Turned or sprained ankles need to be elevated, cooled, and wrapped in a compression bandage to minimize swelling and stiffness. Severe swelling and discoloration will require evacuation and treatment by medical personnel.

cool water

compression bandage

dry bag

paddle float

If you are unsure if the ankle is fractured rather than sprained, you can use a paddle float as an air splint to stabilize the injury while you seek medical assistance. Gently place the foot inside the float bladder and inflate slowly until the joint is stabilized. The float should not cut off circulation or place the ankle in an awkward position. Large feet and small paddle floats make it impossible to use this method.

BACKACHES

Long hours in the cockpit of a kayak can cause some aching backs at the end of the day. Add to this the lack of back support in a typical campsite and you have the makings for some real discomfort. Good posture while paddling helps reduce the strain on your lower back, as does a good system of support for your lower body. Make sure your seatback is providing support and cinch it up so it supports you in an upright position while you're paddling. Make sure your foot braces are positioned so that your lower body assumes a comfortable diamond position with your heels pointed toward the center of the boat. Keeping your legs straight will place more demands on your lower back. Scrounge whatever back support is available at the campsite (claim the only tree, or pout until you get the camp lounger).

Before you resume paddling in the morning, make sure to gently stretch your lower back. Bend over with your knees slightly bent and allow your upper body to dangle (do not bob). Slowly straighten and try to imagine each vertebrae falling into place. When you're in your boat, use your paddle to leverage a lower-back stretch: hold the paddle shaft squared and in front of your torso; now swing your torso and paddle shaft to the side of the boat and continue to face the shaft while you lower the forward blade until it catches the side of the boat. Gently press outward with your rear (aft) hand and feel the stretch across your lower back. Do this on both sides of the boat.

Stretch your lower back numerous times over the course of the day while still in your boat by doing this stretch. While paddling, try to avoid slumping and make sure your seatback is adjusted for the best support and comfort. An inflatable lumbar pad may be used to ease back strain while paddling.

You should also get into the habit of hugging your boat every morning once you're settled in the cockpit. Your back will appreciate the stretch, and your boat will feel reassured.

NUMB FEET

It's very common for kayakers to develop numbness in their feet over the course of a day's paddling. Occasionally this will affect the lower legs and even cause shooting pains up the backs of the legs. Prevention is the key to avoiding this situation. Make sure to wiggle your toes, stretch your ankles, and swing your knees in and out from the centerline of the boat during a day of paddling. Too often, kayakers forget to move their lower body while paddling, and their feet begin to go numb.

Make sure your foot braces are properly adjusted. If they're too short, your ankles will be forced into an uncomfortable bend; if they're too long, you will stress your lower back as you have to straighten your legs to reach the pedals. Check the seat base in your kayak. It is helpful to have a slight lift to the forward edge of the seat, taking pressure off the backs of the legs and allowing the pelvis to tilt forward into a better position for paddling. In general, the seat

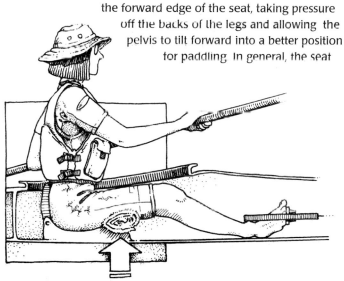

Numb feet are common and can often be avoided by making sure the seat lip is tilted up and supports the backs of the thighs. Remember to wiggle your toes and move your legs around over the course of the day. Too often, paddlers forget to stretch and move their lower body while paddling.

should support the backs of your legs in a position that is several inches above level. If numbness in lower extremities is a constant problem, your seat base angle may be the culprit. In the field, you can place a rolled towel beneath your upper thighs or place an inflatable pad off the forward edge of your seat. You can create a permanent fix at home with blocks of Minicel foam shaped and glued into place.

HEAT AND COLD

SUNBURN

Sunburn in a sandy, salty environment can be particularly painful. Every little piece of grit feels like a rasp against your skin. Of course, prevention is the best strategy. You should always slather yourself with sunscreen of SPF 30 or higher and replenish it over the course of the day. Make sure to cover sensitive areas like the tops of ears and backs of arms. Sunlight can reflect off the water and the deck of your boat and cook areas you never think to protect, like under your chin. A wide-brimmed hat and a lightweight shirt will help protect you from the sun's rays and be useful after you get off the water.

If you can spare the freshwater, gently flush your sunburned skin to remove any grit and salt deposits. You can apply a topical anesthetic like a lidocaine ointment that will temporarily ease the burning sensation. Aloe and vitamin E gels tend to feel cool and soothing and will help moisturize the skin and aid the healing process. Whenever these sunburned areas get wet, reapply moisturizer. When you face the sun again, you'll need to be very careful about protecting yourself with a hat and liberal amounts of sunscreen.

Don't wait until you feel the burn—protect your skin with fabric and lots of sunscreen while under way. Any sunburn will need to be flushed with freshwater and kept moisturized. Particular care will need to be taken to further protect sunburned skin while under way.

DEHYDRATION

Sea kayakers are notorious for getting dehydrated. Peeing while under way is a hassle, and we figure we'll wait until the lunch break or the end of the day to tank up on liquids. This is not a smart way to plan a day of paddling. You should be draining a water bottle at least every couple of hours while under way and even more frequently in hot, dry climates.

You cannot afford to get dehydrated during a kayak trip. You will get weak and lethargic and be more prone to getting cold or suffering heat exhaustion. Make sure you keep downing water over the entire day. If you feel even a tinge of a headache coming on, drink even more water. Plan frequent breaks from paddling and make sure all group members are draining their water bottles. Refill everyone's water bottles before you resume paddling.

You should consume a typical 20- to 24-ounce water bottle every hour or so while under way, especially if you are paddling in hot, dry climates. If you feel any lightheadedness or a headache coming on, you are not drinking enough water.

HYPOTHERMIA

More often than not, kayaking fatalities have been the result of hypothermia or drownings caused by hypothermia. Many popular paddling spots are in cold water that can chill the body into lethargy and even death if immersion continues. The best way to avoid hypothermia is to dress for the water temperatures, not the air temperatures. On a sunny, warm day in May it's often hard to remember that the water may still be a shocking fifty degrees.

Just being damp and exposed to wind can bring on the first stages of hypothermia. Keep an eye out for early signs of hypothermia in your paddling group. As the body begins to cool, shivering occurs to generate heat. Vasoconstriction occurs as surface blood vessels minimize the heat loss from the skin, causing goose bumps. Hands and feet might become clumsy, and a mildly hypothermic person may begin to stumble and drop things or may be slow to respond to a question or direction. If you notice a general sense of lethargy, warm the person immediately. Begin adding layers of warm clothing and providing protection from the wind. Have the victim consume warm, sweet liquids like cocoa or gelatin (follow instructions on box). If he has gotten wet, get him dry or at the very least swathed in a windproof outer layer until you can get him into dry clothing. Make sure he is wearing a warm hat.

Most instances of hypothermia involve these early stages that can be remedied with quick attention to the problem. Be conservative in your assessment of hypothermia. Do not let a group member shrug off help if you suspect he is indeed cold.

Hypothermia is a very serious threat to kayakers. A hypothermic paddler must be kept dry and warmed quickly. A hypo-wrap can be made with fleece blankets surrounded with a space blanket on an insulating ground pad (a sleeping bag can also be used). Cover the head to avoid more heat loss.

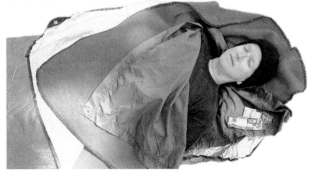

Often a mildly hypothermic person will refuse help and then slip into a lethargy that can cause him to capsize or chill down even faster. If the person is not responding to initial attempts to warm him, he should be stripped and placed in a pre-warmed sleeping bag with hot water bottles or another group member who can supply his own body warmth.

If the victim does not respond to rewarming within minutes, contact emergency personnel and arrange evacuation. Rewarming procedures for an acutely hypothermic person can trigger shock and are best done in a controlled hospital setting.

HYPERTHERMIA

If your body becomes dehydrated and unable to cool itself properly, the stress on the body can lead to heat exhaustion and eventually to heat stroke. The first signs of overheating are a flushed appearance of the skin caused by blood vessels that have dilated and are close to the surface of the skin. The person is usually, but not always, sweating profusely. If a group member begins to feel lightheaded, dizzy, or nauseous, she should lie down and elevate her feet. Make sure she consumes copious amounts of water (at least 1 to 2 quarts). Keep her still and hydrated until her normal color returns and all signs of overheating have disappeared.

Heat stroke, which represents the complete breakdown of the body's heat regulation, is a true emergency. The body's core temperature rises rapidly, and the victim loses the ability to sweat. She may become confused and lapse into unconsciousness quickly. You must get her into a shady spot and allow as much air circulation as possible while cooling her with wet clothing and dousing her with cool water. Contact emergency personnel and begin plans for evacuation; the victim will probably need to be put on intravenous solutions.

Douse yourself with water and dampen a hat or bandanna regularly in hot climates. Take special care to stay hydrated and seek shade if you are feeling lightheaded.

NATURE'S OFFERINGS

SALTWATER RASHES

These rashes are usually the result of salt water chafing on sensitive skin or of entrapped sweat glands that are further irritated by saltwater deposits on the skin. They can be red and itchy and very sensitive to the touch. Clean the area with freshwater and dry with a soft piece of material. Apply a cortisone ointment (over-the-counter strength) to the area every six hours or so.

If the rash is under the arm or around the ankle where a fabric seam continues to rub, protect the surface of the skin with a layer of clothing if possible. A soft, clean thermal underwear top or bottom will often protect a chafed spot from the ravages of a wet suit seam rub. Continue to treat the area with cortisone ointment and flush with freshwater.

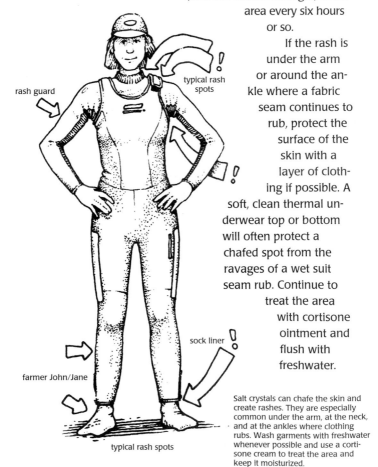

rash guard

typical rash spots

sock liner

farmer John/Jane

typical rash spots

Salt crystals can chafe the skin and create rashes. They are especially common under the arm, at the neck, and at the ankles where clothing rubs. Wash garments with freshwater whenever possible and use a cortisone cream to treat the area and keep it moisturized.

BARNACLE CUTS

These little cuts and abrasions can be painful and continue to plague you throughout a multiday trip if you don't clean them thoroughly. Barnacle cuts often occur when you place a hand on a rock to hold the boat in position or to get in and out. These nasty cuts can prevent you from paddling if they flare into full-scale infections, so treat them quickly and thoroughly.

Clean the wounds with soapy water and then treat with hydrogen peroxide to insure that no fragments are left on the skin. Apply an antibacterial ointment and put a Steri-Strip or some other clean bandage over the wound to protect it. Repeat this treatment at the end of each paddling day until the wound has healed.

DEER TICKS

Deer ticks are very difficult to detect, unlike their larger cousins, the dog or wood tick. They may be no larger than a pinhead in their nymphal stage when they are most likely to transmit the spirochete that causes Lyme disease, a serious illness. A deer tick may appear only as a small brown dot resembling a freckle or speck of dirt and so go unnoticed for days. It normally takes about 36 hours for the deer tick to transmit the disease to a human, so a daily inspection is important. Lyme disease can be debilitating, so any bite from a deer tick must be followed by testing for the presence of Lyme disease.

If you travel in areas where deer ticks are present, you should check yourself thoroughly at the end of each day.

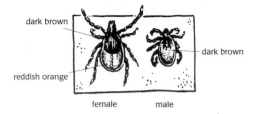

dark brown

dark brown

reddish orange

female   male

Adult Deer Tick *(Ixodes scapularis/dammini)*

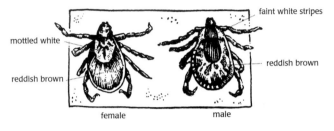

faint white stripes

mottled white

reddish brown

reddish brown

female   male

Adult Dog Tick *(Dermacentor variabillis)*

These ticks love to hide in hard-to-spot places, so you'll need a hand mirror to check every crack and crevice (yes, every one). Even if you do not spot a deer tick, check your skin for any sign of a deer tick bite, usually a telltale red halo around the bite. If you find the tick, remove it with tweezers (pull, don't squeeze) and save it in a small vial to give to medical personnel (your physician or the closest emergency room) for testing.

Since deer ticks are found only on land, you can help protect yourself from them by keeping your feet, ankles, and lower legs covered when you walk through areas where they have been reported. They tend to favor brushy areas and spruce forests but may be found anywhere there is a deer population. Check with local outfitters about the threat of deer ticks in your planned paddling area.

RED TIDE

Red tide is a bloom in the population of single-celled dinoflagellates that occurs in the intertidal zone. These organisms are absorbed by other marine organisms like mussels and clams and can be toxic to humans as paralytic shellfish poison (PSP). NOAA weather radio reports red tide closings, and you should note the locations of these areas on your chart. Never forage for mussels or clams if you are unsure of the water quality or the presence of red tide. Paralytic shellfish poisoning can be fatal.

Even if you feel confident that any shellfish you collect are free of these organisms, try rubbing a piece of the meat on your inner lip. If you experience any tingling, consider the shellfish suspect and do not eat them. Don't depend on this test in the absence of any other information about the presence of red tide in your paddling area—only as a backup check.

BROWN-TAIL MOTHS

These fairly nondescript moths are common to many coastal areas along the East Coast. The caterpillars of the brown-tail moth produce tiny hairs that are airborne and can create strong and potentially dangerous allergic reactions in humans. Reported cases have included everything from mild itching and rashes to serious respiratory problems. The caterpillars are active during the popular paddling months of June through August.

It's best to find out ahead of time whether brown-tail moths have been reported in the area you plan to explore. Their presence is not something you can easily detect once you go

These moths have come and gone from East Coast sites over the past two hundred years and now are on the rise in many popular paddling areas. They are nondescript but the tiny hairs on brown-tail moth caterpillars can be a serious problem. Skin irritations and respiratory problems may occur.

ashore, and by then it may be too late if the hairs are present and airborne. Contact local outfitters or water trail organizations for information about their presence. If you're prone to asthma or respiratory problems, be conservative in your planning and avoid all suspected areas.

POISONOUS PLANTS

Poison ivy and poison oak thrive in many coastal areas, blanketing the ground or even growing around large trees. Just paddling by these spots can make you begin to itch! Any wilderness traveler should know how to identify common

poison ivy

poisonous plants; if you know they're around, you can avoid them.

Exposure to poisonous plants produces a reaction that is usually noticeable within a day or so after exposure. Small red blisters may appear and be very itchy and sensitive to the touch. Clean the area, and any other areas you suspect were exposed, with warm, soapy water. Cover with a cortisone cream and refrain from scratching, which further irritates the area. Other over-the-counter creams like calamine lotion may help keep the itching to a minimum. If the blisters begin to weep and swell, or if you are prone to severe reactions to these plants, seek medical help.

poison oak

FREQUENT COMPLAINTS

BLISTERS

Thankfully, sea kayakers are not as prone to blisters as hikers and backpackers, but we may occasionally experience them on our hands and feet. A blister on the hand will usually occur between the thumb and index finger where the paddle shaft rides during a normal paddle grip. A death grip on the paddle will only aggravate this problem, so try to maintain a relaxed grip. Since as paddlers our hands are almost always wet, our skin can get soft and is easily abraded as a paddle shaft twists back and forth thousands of times a day. Salt crystals add to the abrasiveness, and friction blisters may develop.

Unless the area between your thumb and index finger is already callused from years of paddling, try coating it with a dab of aloe gel to keep it lubricated and decrease the friction on this spot. Some paddlers use moleskin or Spenco Second Skin if a blister begins to develop. Moleskin is also useful if you grind your outside heel into the bottom of the boat (especially in composite boats). Placing a patch on these rubbed areas may prevent a full blister from forming.

If you develop a blister, you may need to drain it to avoid infection. You must get the area as clean as possible with warm, soapy water or Betadine and then lance it with a sterile needle or scalpel. Drain the fluid from the blister, apply an antibiotic cream, and cover with a sterile dressing. Continue to clean and reapply antibiotic cream until the area heals. If the area becomes inflamed or shows signs of infection, seek medical help.

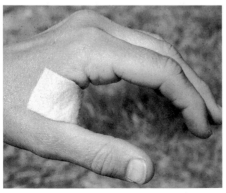

Catching blisters before they begin to form is the best practice. If you feel a hot spot developing, treat immediately so you don't end up with a full-blown problem that might affect your trip.

BURNS

The immediate response to a burn should be to immerse it in cold water. Luckily, sea kayakers are surrounded by plenty of water that is often cold. The best treatment is to place the burn under fresh ice water until you can feel it cool. This will also remove any charred fabric or the remains of any solvents on the skin. Burns are classified as first, second, or third degree and their treatment depends on the severity and extent of the injury. Extensive burns or third-degree burns must be seen by trained medical personnel. It is too difficult to maintain a sterile environment and continue treatment of severe burns in a wilderness setting, so the victim must be evacuated.

First- and second-degree burns that are not extensive (covering less than 10 percent of the body) can be treated after the area has been cooled and rinsed in cold water. Clean the area with soap and water and rinse thoroughly. First-degree burns are superficial burns that show redness but remain dry. Treat

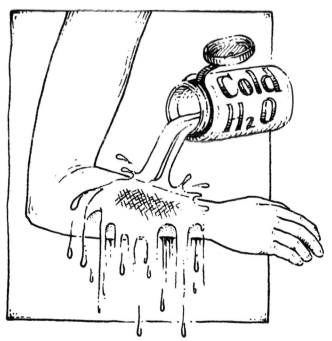

Superficial burns should be immediately cooled and then flushed with freshwater and cleaned. Monitor burns closely for infection and keep the area clean and moisturized. Extensive burns or third-degree burns should always be treated as soon as possible by medical personnel.

these with a burn ointment, which will deaden the pain and keep the skin moisturized. A first-degree burn should heal in about three days.

Second-degree burns show moist areas and begin to form blisters with a reddened base. Cool and treat the area as you would for a first-degree burn but take great care to monitor any additional swelling or redness, indicating an infection. Dead skin on the wound usually dries and sloughs off after several days, but the entire wound may require as much as two weeks to heal.

You can use burn dressings for both first- and second-degree burns. The damage of third-degree burns reaches the subcutaneous layer and may show charring and discoloration. These burns are very serious and can send the injured person into shock; seek medical help immediately.

CONTACT LENS PROBLEMS

Sea kayaking can be rough on contact lenses. Consider always wearing a pair of sunglasses or goggles to protect your lenses when paddling if the weather or water is rough. Wind may fold over a soft contact lens in your eye and make it easy to lose. Wearing side protectors on your sunglasses will help keep wind from funneling across the surface of the eye and wreaking havoc on your lenses.

Protect your eyes from splashes and wind with goggles or sunglasses with side shields. Salt water and saltwater-saturated air can irritate eyes and cause dryness in contact lens wearers.

A direct hit in the face from spray has been known to wash a contact lens from the eye. If you're lucky you'll find it on the front of your life vest or sprayskirt where you can grab it before it's washed overboard. Always carry a spare pair of lenses or backup prescription glasses and lots of extra saline solution. You'll probably find that your lenses need cleaning at least every day, and salt spray may make your eyes sensitive and drier than usual. Glasses of any type should always have a retainer strap in place, preferably a floating one.

Index

Numbers in **bold** refer to pages
with illustrations